It's no crime to save time

Cover art: Kevin Klein
Divider page design: Allison Cease
Author: Marcella Richman

**Owned and Distribed by
The Three Bears Honey Co.
908 63rd Ave. N.
Moorhead, MN 56560
218-236-5933**

Our Standard Abbreviations

tsp.	-	teaspoon
T.	-	tablespoon
c.	-	cup
oz.	-	ounce or ounces
lb.	-	pound or pounds
sq.	-	square
ctn.	-	carton or container
pkg.	-	package(s)
btl.	-	bottle(s)
liter	-	liter
approx.	-	approximately
temp.	-	temperature
sm.	-	small
med.	-	medium
lg.	-	large
pt.	-	pint
qt.	-	quart
doz.	-	dozen
bu.	-	bushel
env.	-	envelope(s)
pkt.	-	packet(s)
mg	-	milligram(s)
gm	-	gram(s)
gal.	-	gallon(s)

> Order blanks are included in back of book for your convenience.

ISBN: 09642215-2-7
All rights reserved
Copyright: 2004 Marcella Richman

First Printing - June 2004
Last Printing - August 2010

Printed by:

JUMBO JACK'S COOKBOOKS
AUDUBON MEDIA CORPORATION
301 BROADWAY • AUDUBON, IA 50025
1-800-798-2635

ACKNOWLEDGMENTS

Never mind the old adage, "Too many cooks spoil the broth"! In compiling a cookbook, many good cooks improve the mix! To all of you who took the time and made the effort to share your favorite recipes, a generous thank you. The large volume of responses is proof enough that, no matter how busy, many of you still practice your kitchen talents. And because of your generosity, another cookbook made from scratch, is ready to serve.

Aside from the recipes handed to me, mailed, e-mailed, or phoned, a considerable number were also used from sources nearby, the daily paper, magazines, and my bulging collection of cookbooks. Every attempt was made to give credit where credit is due.

Several volumes were very helpful in supplying the quotes, proverbs, or hints that add an extra dash of flavor to the make-up of this book. Credits go to: John Louis Anderson's <u>German Humor</u>, Perennial Library, Harper and Row; <u>The Golfer's Book of Wisdom</u>, by Criswell Freeman, Walnut Grove Press, Nashville, TN; <u>The Quotable Book Lover</u> by Jacobs and Hjalmarsson, Lyons Press; <u>Simple Abundance</u> by Sarah Ban Breathnach, Warner Book, Inc, NY; Joanne Asala's collection: <u>Swedish Proverbs</u>, Penfield Press, Iowa City, IA; and <u>The Dairy</u> by Anna Nicholas, Grange Books, London.

Notes & Recipes

Table of Contents

Start Your Engines –
   Appetizers, Snacks & Drinks 1-26

Brake for Breads & Brunch 27-56

Speedway Salads & Sides 57-76

Put the Pedal to the Kettle –
   Meats & Main Dishes 77-122

Fuel Stop – Cookies & Bars 123-150

Finish Line – Desserts 151-192

Tips & Tune-Ups 193-204

Index 205-210

FAVORITE RECIPES
FROM MY COOKBOOK

Recipe Name	Page Number

Start Your Engines - Appetizers, Snacks & Drinks

Notes & Recipes

Start Your Engines – Appetizers, Snacks & Drinks

Adult Root Beer Floats*

In a blender, place:
4 ice cubes	6 oz. club soda

Blend 30 seconds.
Add:
8 oz. Phillips Root Beer Schnapps	2 scoops vanilla ice cream

Blend for another 30 seconds. Pour into tall frosty glass. Enjoy an adult summer cooler.

Ann Cease via Laine Larson

Almond Candy

1 c. Flavorite blanched slivered almonds	1/2 c. Flavorite granulated sugar
1/2 c. Flavorite butter or margarine	1 T. corn syrup

Line bottom and sides of an 8- or 9-inch cake pan with aluminum foil (not plastic wrap or waxed paper). Butter foil heavily; reserve. Combine blanched slivered almonds, butter or margarine, sugar and corn syrup in 10-inch skillet. Bring to a boil over medium heat, stirring constantly. Boil, stirring constantly, until mixture turns golden brown, about 5 or 6 minutes. Working quickly, spread candy in prepared pan. Cool about 15 minutes, or until firm. Remove candy from pan by lifting edges of foil. Peel off foil. Cool thoroughly. Yield: about 3/4 pound.

From: Flavorite Almond package

Artichoke Dip*

2 (14 oz.) cans artichoke hearts (rinse, squeeze & chop)	1/2 c. Miracle Whip
2 c. shredded Parmesan cheese	1 sm. onion, chopped

May be mixed ahead of time. Bake at 350° for 30 minutes in a small glass dish that can be used for serving. Serve hot with your favorite chips.

Paula Wright

Buttermilk Shake*

1 pt. vanilla frozen yogurt or
　ice milk
1 c. buttermilk
1 tsp. grated lemon peel
1/2 tsp. vanilla extract
1 drop lemon extract

Place all ingredients into blender. Cover and process on high until smooth. Pour into glasses. Refrigerate any leftovers. Yield: 2 servings.

Colleen Clancy

Candied Pecans*

2 1/2 c. pecan halves
1 c. sugar
1/2 c. cream (no substitutions)
1/4 c. butter (no substitutions)
1 tsp. vanilla
1 T. Karo syrup (opt.)

Cook 10 minutes. Pour in pecans and mix until creamy. Put on waxed paper to cool.

Margaret Perry

Caramel Popcorn*

1 stick margarine
1/2 c. brown sugar
8 lg. marshmallows

Cook together until marshmallows are melted. Pour over 2 quarts of popped corn.

Christine C. Worthen

Chocolate Fudge*

1 lg. bag Toll-House chocolate
　chips
1 lg. bag butterscotch chips
1 (14 oz.) can Eagle Brand milk
1 T. vanilla
1 c. chopped walnuts
1/2 stick margarine

Put all ingredients in microwave-safe dish. Melt, stirring occasionally. When thoroughly melted and blended, pour into a buttered pan. Chill. Cut. Serve.

So easy – so good!

Doris Goberville

Cinnamon Trail Mix*

2 c. toasted oat cereal
2 c. hexagon-shaped corn cereal
2 c. pretzel bits
3/4 c. raisins
1/2 c. sunflower seeds
2 T. reduced-fat margarine
2 T. brown sugar
1 T. cinnamon

In a large bowl, combine the cereals, pretzel bits, raisins and sunflower seeds. Toss gently. Melt margarine in a microwave or saucepan and stir in brown sugar and cinnamon. Pour over the cereal mixture. Toss to coat. Bake 8 to 10 minutes in a 350° oven.

From: Best of the Best Great Plains Cookbook

Crab Dip*

1 (16 oz.) ctn. sour cream
1 can crab meat, drained (save juice)
Onion salt
Garlic salt
4 drops Worcestershire sauce

Mix all together. Add about 1/8-cup crab juice. Refrigerate until ready to serve with corn chips.

Vi Egan

Crab-Filled Mini Popovers*

1 beaten egg
1 slightly-beaten egg white
3/4 c. milk
1 T. cooking oil
3/4 c. flour
1/4 tsp. dried dill weed
Dash of salt
1 pt. deli crabmeat salad

Generously grease 24 (1 3/4-inch) muffin cups. In a medium bowl, combine beaten egg, slightly beaten egg white, milk and oil. Add flour, dried dill weed and dash of salt. Beat until smooth. Fill muffin cups half-full. Bake in a 400° oven for 20 minutes, or until light brown. Do not open oven during baking. Remove popovers from pans and cool slightly. Chop 1 pint deli crabmeat salad. Cut a slit in the side of each popover and fill with a rounded teaspoon of crabmeat salad. Place on baking sheet and bake in 400° oven for 5 minutes or more, or until heated through. Yield: 24.

Cathy Cornell

Cranberry Trail Mix*

1/4 c. butter
1/4 c. brown sugar
1 T. maple syrup
1/2 tsp. cinnamon
1 tsp. curry powder
1 1/2 c. dried cranberries
1 1/2 c. coarsely-chopped walnuts or slivered almonds
1 1/2 c. pretzel nuggets

Preheat oven to 300°. Melt butter and brown sugar in large pot over medium heat. Stir in spices. Add the rest; stir to combine. Spread onto greased pan. Bake 15 minutes, or until crunchy and lightly browned.
I'm often asked for this recipe when I serve this yummy treat.

Laura Schock

Cream Cheese Roll-Ups*

1 (8 oz.) pkg. cream cheese
4 oz. sour cream
1/4 c. chopped black olives
1/2 c. grated cheese
Flour tortillas
Lunchmeat of your choice

Combine cream cheese, sour cream, black olives and cheese. Mix well. Spread mixture on tortillas. Put lunchmeat on and roll up. Place in refrigerator and chill for 1 hour. Cut into 1-inch pieces (slices) and serve.

Jenni Richman

Crispy Cheese Crackers*

1 1/4 c. grated Cheddar cheese
1 c. flour
1/2 c. butter
1 tsp. chopped chives
1/2 tsp. salt
2 T. sesame seeds (for tops)
3 T. flake salt (for tops)

In large bowl, combine cheese, flour and butter (cut in small chunks). Add chives and salt about halfway through mixing process. Once dough holds together, form into rolls about 1 inch in diameter. Wrap in plastic wrap, then foil. Refrigerate overnight or store in freezer. Slice thin (1/8-inch) and place on greased cookie pans. Sprinkle with sesame seeds. Bake at 425° for 8 to 10 minutes. Serve warm or room temperature. Yield: about 4 dozen crackers.
Preparation time: 15 minutes.

Judith Krueger

Broiled Crab Melt-Aways*

6 English muffins, split
1/2 c., or less, margarine
2 T. mayonnaise
1 (6 1/2 to 7 oz.) can crabmeat
1 (5 oz.) jar Old English cheese
1/4 tsp. garlic salt

Mix margarine, mayonnaise, crabmeat, cheese and garlic salt. Spread on muffins. Cut into quarters. Freeze on cookie sheet. Store in zip-lock bags. Use as needed.
To serve: Broil on cookie sheet on middle to lower rack until bubbly and puffy and slightly brown. Yield: 48 appetizers.

Donna Dewald

Delicious Shrimp Dip*

2 (6 oz.) cans sm. shrimp, drained
1 (8 oz.) pkg. cream cheese
1/2 sm. onion, grated
2 T. ketchup
1 T. horseradish
Salt & pepper, to taste

Combine all ingredients and stir together. Refrigerate for 4 hours before serving with crackers. If dip is too thick, add more ketchup.

From: American Profile

Deviled Eggs with Sour Cream and Salmon Roe

Domestic golden whitefish roe, much of which comes from the Great Lakes region, can also be used.

24 lg. hard-boiled eggs, peeled & halved lengthwise
2/3 c. fat-free sour cream
1/3 c. low-fat mayonnaise
1/4 c. chopped fresh chives
1 T. Dijon mustard
2 tsp. fresh lemon juice
3/4 tsp. salt
1/2 tsp. ground black pepper
1 (4 oz.) jar salmon roe or golden whitefish roe

Carefully scoop yolks from egg halves into large bowl. Finely-chop 4 egg-white halves; add to bowl with yolks. Add sour cream and next 6 ingredients to yolks. Mash with fork until smooth. Arrange egg-white halves on large platter. Spoon filling into each, mounding slightly. (Should be prepared 2 hours ahead. Cover and refrigerate.) Garnish each egg half with 1/4 teaspoon roe and serve.
My buddy Chris sent this one (I would use actual caviar or Japanese flying fish roe).

Tom Lopez

Don's Popcorn Balls*

1 c. brown sugar, packed
1/2 c. water
1/4 tsp. salt
1/4 tsp. cream of tartar
1 T. vinegar

Mix and boil for 10 minutes over medium heat. Then add 2 tablespoons butter. Continue boiling to hard ball stage. Add 1/2 tablespoon vanilla. Pour over popped corn and form into balls.

Joyce Baldwin

Dreamy Fruit Dip*

1 (8 oz.) pkg. cream cheese, softened
1/2 c. butter or margarine, softened
1/2 c. marshmallow creme
1 (8 oz.) ctn. frozen whipped topping, thawed
Assorted fresh fruit

In a small mixing bowl, beat cream cheese and butter until smooth. Beat in marshmallow creme. Fold in whipped topping. Serve with fruit. Store in the refrigerator. Yield: about 4 cups.
Ready in 15 minutes or less.
Offer alongside apple wedges, pineapple chunks and grapes. Chill leftover dip for a tasty topping for toast the next morning.

Anna Beiler

Easy Homemade Freezer Jam

7 c. cut-up rhubarb
6 oz. red Jello (raspberry or strawberry)
5 c. sugar
10 oz. frozen raspberries or strawberries

Mix sugar and rhubarb; let stand until juicy (2 to 3 hours). Cook until tender and comes to a boil. Remove from heat; add the Jello and frozen berries. Cook again until it comes to a rolling boil. Put into sterile jars and seal. Keep in freezer; after open, keep refrigerated.

Diane Kohler

Easy Way Pizza Rolls

Buy pizza rolls. Cook in the microwave.

Joyce Lambert

Fairway Fuel*

Mix all together. Put in zip baggie for a good golf day.

1/2 c. black or white raisins
1/2 c. dried bananas
1/2 c. dried apples
1/2 c. dried apricots
1 c. plain M&M's
1/2 c. dry roasted peanuts

*From: Golf for Women,
Oct. 1993*

Fast Fudge*

1 pt. ice cream
2 lb. (any kind) chocolate

Let the ice cream melt in a large mixing bowl. In the microwave, melt 2 pounds chocolate. It can be chocolate chips, Hershey's bars or almond bark, or any combination to equal 2 pounds. Start mixing the melted ice cream with electric mixer and drizzle in the melted chocolate as you're mixing. When all the chocolate is mixed in, pour fudge into a buttered 9x13-inch pan.

*Deb Tuck,
Karol McCracken*

Green Olive Cheese Ball*

1 (8 oz.) pkg. shredded Co-Jack cheese
1 (8 oz.) pkg. shredded mild Cheddar cheese
1 sm. jar chopped green olives, drained
1 sm. jar Cheez Whiz
Garnish: 1 jar whole green olives with pimentos

Combine all ingredients. Press mixture into any bowl or mold that has been lined with clear wrap. Turn upside-down on plate. Peel off wrap. Cut whole green olives in half and garnish outside of cheese ball. Serve on crackers.
Preparation time: 10 minutes.
May double in size by using 16-ounce packages cheese and large jar Cheez Whiz and large jar of olives.

Brenda O'Brien

Grilled Tuna Sandwich*

1 (6 oz.) can tuna
2 slices American cheese
4 slices bread
2 sm. dill pickles
4 tsp. mayonnaise
4 tsp. catsup (opt.)
2 tsp. butter or margarine

Drain tuna. Slice dill pickles lengthwise 1/8-inch thick. Spread mayonnaise on 1 slice of bread. Catsup can also add a bit of zest. Layer well-drained tuna over this. Add a slice of American cheese, then sliced dill pickle evenly placed. Top with a slice of bread. Spread outside of sandwich with butter or margarine and grill both sides until lightly browned. Yield: 2 sandwiches.

Jacob Severson

Hot Reuben Dip*

1 lg. can sauerkraut
4 or 5 pkg. corned beef
16 oz. Swiss cheese, shredded
1 c. thousand island dressing

Mix and heat in 1 1/2-quart crock-pot on low heat until hot. Serve with crackers.
Note: Can do half recipe.
I like to use Triscuit Original crackers.

Loretta Birdeno

Hot Spinach Artichoke Dip

1 (8 oz.) pkg. Philadelphia cream cheese, softened
1 (14 oz.) can artichoke hearts, drained, chopped
1 (10 oz.) pkg. chopped spinach, thawed, drained frozen spinach
1/2 c. Kraft mayonnaise
1/2 c. Kraft grated Parmesan cheese
1 clove garlic, minced

Beat cream cheese and mayonnaise with mixer on medium speed until well blended. Add remaining ingredients; mix well. Spoon into 9-inch pie plate or quiche dish. Bake at 350° for 20 to 25 minutes, until lightly browned. Garnish with chopped tomato. Serve with crackers or as vegetable dip. Yield: 16 servings.

From: Philadelphia Cream Cheese wrapper

Ice Cream Fudge*

1 lb. almond bark
1 lb. chocolate bark
4 c. semi-sweet chocolate chips
1 pt. vanilla ice cream, softened
1 c. chopped pecans

Combine almond bark, chocolate bark and chocolate chips in buttered 9x13-inch baking dish. Melt in 250° oven; stir to mix well. Stir in ice cream and pecans. Let stand until cool. Cut into squares. May omit pecans or substitute other nuts for pecans.

Sylvia Fust Hansen

Easy Marble Bark*

6 sq. Baker's semi-sweet chocolate
1 pkg. (6 sq.) Baker's white premium chocolate
1 c. toasted chopped nuts or Baker's Angel Flake coconut

Microwave the semi-sweet chocolate and the white chocolate in separate bowls. Stir until completely melted. Stir 1/2 cup of the nuts or coconut into each bowl. Alternately spoon melted chocolates onto waxed paper-lined cookie sheet or tray. Swirl chocolates together with knife to marbleize. Refrigerate 1 hour, until firm. Break into pieces. Yield: about 1 pound.

From: Baker's wrapper

Jutta's Easy Dip*

3 sm. tomatoes, cut in pieces
1 can green chilies, cut & chopped
1 can chopped black olives
1/2 lg. onion (or 1 sm.), finely chopped

Mix.
Add:
3 T. cider vinegar
1 T. oil
Salt & pepper, or seasoning of your choice

Jutta Jai,
Melva Glemming

Mexican Artichoke Dip*
An old favorite with a Southwestern twist.

1 c. fat-free mayonnaise	1/8 tsp. garlic powder
1/2 c. Parmesan cheese, grated	2 (14 oz.) cans artichoke hearts,
1 c. soft bread crumbs	drained & finely chopped
1/4 tsp. Worcestershire sauce	1 (14 oz.) can chopped green chilies
1/4 tsp. hot pepper sauce	Cooking spray

Preheat oven to 350°. Combine mayonnaise, Parmesan cheese, bread crumbs, Worcestershire sauce, hot pepper sauce and garlic powder. Gently fold in artichokes and green chilies. Spoon mixture into a 1-quart casserole dish coated with cooking spray. Cover and bake for 20 minutes. Serve with pita wedges, melba rounds or vegetable sticks. Yield: 13 1/2 cups (14 servings); servings size: 1/4 cup.

Preparation time: 15 minutes. Cooking time: 12 to 20 minutes.

Microwave instructions: Microwave on MEDIUM (50% POWER) for 12 to 14 minutes, stirring halfway through cooking time.

Note: Fat-free mayonnaise can be substituted for regular mayonnaise in highly-flavored salads, dips and on sandwiches. However, cooking with it may not produce the same quality product as you might expect. To be safe, follow recipes, such as this one that have been tested using fat-free mayonnaise.

Doris Sauerland

Millionaire's Candy*

1 (14 oz.) pkg. caramels	2 c. pecan pieces
4 scant T. milk	1/4 bar paraffin
1 (12 oz.) pkg. chocolate chips	Butter

Melt caramels in milk over very low heat. Add pecans. Drop by teaspoonfuls onto buttered waxed paper. Chill. Melt paraffin and chocolate chips in heavy saucepan over low heat. Dip candy into chocolate paraffin mixture and return to waxed paper. Chill.

Ann Cease,
From: Northern Lights magazine

Never loan money to a baker if his only collateral is sauerkraut.
John Louis Anderson

Microwave Caramel Corn*

10 to 12 c. popped corn (make popcorn before making syrup)

1 stick butter
1/4 c. corn syrup
1 c. brown sugar

Combine in bowl and microwave to boiling. Stir. Cook 3 more minutes. Stir in 1/4 teaspoon baking soda and 1 teaspoon vanilla.

Put popped corn in large brown paper bag. Pour hot mixture over this. Fold down top of bag about 3 folds. Shake well. Microwave 1 1/2 minutes, shaking every 30 seconds. Open sack. Cool. *Ginny Schobinger*

Nacho Sauce*

2 lb. ground beef
Salt & pepper
1 c. water
2 cans Cheddar cheese soup
1/2 c. chopped onion
1 pkg. taco seasoning
1 lb. Velveeta
1 sm. jar jalapeño Cheez Whiz

Brown ground beef with onion. Drain. Add taco seasoning and water. Simmer until dry. Take off burner and add Velveeta. Melt. Add soup and Cheez Whiz. Stir until melted. Serve warm with chips. May be kept warm in crock-pot. Can be frozen. *Pam Walcker*

North Dakota Guacamole*

3 to 5 lg. ripe Hass avocados (do not be fooled by flavorless Florida-grown avocados – for that big avocado flavor you've got to go to California)
Cilantro, finely chopped
2 bunches finely-chopped green onions
Village brand Extra-Hot Salsa (this product would be labeled extra-mild in 47 of the other 50 states)
Fat-free sour cream
1 lime

Smoosh up the avocados in a large bowl; add plenty of salt and pepper. Stir in green onions and plenty of cilantro (be sure to chop both up finely – this opens the flavor). Stir in most of your Village Extra-Hot Salsa (but it's really mild, honest), making sure the consistency remains thick. Stir in 2 or 3 heaping tablespoons of sour cream, depending on how successful you were at locating ripe avocados. Squeeze in half a lime and stir up some more. Place the avocado pits on top, cover bowl with plastic shrink-wrap and leave in the refrigerator for at least an hour prior to serving. Before serving, pull out the pits, squeeze in the other half lime; stir again and serve (in addition to adding flavor, the lime retards the avocado's tendency to turn black after sitting out for a while). *Tom Lopez*

Olive-Ham Cheese Ball*

1 (8 oz.) pkg. cream cheese
2 c. finely-shredded Cheddar cheese
2 tsp. Worcestershire sauce
2 tsp. grated onion
1 tsp. mustard
1/2 tsp. paprika
4 T. chopped green olives
1 can deviled ham
Crushed nuts or parsley

Bring cream cheese to room temperature. Whisk with a fork until creamy. Add remaining ingredients. Chill until firm. Roll into 1 or 2 balls or logs. Roll in chopped parsley or nuts. Refrigerate. Will be ready to serve in 1/2 hour.

Donna Johnson,
Jeri Thilmony

Orange Julius*

1/2 c. powdered sugar
1 (6 oz.) can frozen orange juice concentrate
1 c. milk
1 c. water
10 ice cubes
1/2 tsp. vanilla

Put ice cubes through ice crusher or crush by hand. Put all ingredients in blender. Blend on low speed until desired consistency.

Rita M. Halland

Orange Popsicle Drink*

1 scoop (1/4 c.) orange Gatorade
2 scoops (1/2 c.) orange Tang
2 qt. water

Put ingredients into a 2-quart pitcher. Add water; mix. Chill. Yield: 8 (8-ounce) servings.

The scoop measurements are based on the utensil provided by Tang and Gatorade to measure their product. Makes a tasty thirst-quencher. seven-day refrigerator shelf life.

Jacob Severson

No man can be wise on an empty stomach.
George Eliot

Oriental Chicken Wings

4 to 5 lb. chicken wings, cut at the joints, wing tips discarded
3 T. soy sauce
1/2 c. ketchup
1 c. honey
2 T. vegetable oil
1 tsp. minced garlic
1/4 tsp. cayenne pepper (opt.)

Thaw chicken wings and place in a single layer in a 9x13-inch pan or open roaster. Combine the rest of the ingredients to make sauce to pour over the wings. Bake, uncovered, for 1 to 1 1/2 hours at 320°. Yield: 20 to 25 appetizers.
After baking, there will be a lot of sauce.

Coni Horsager

Party Cheese Ball*

8 oz. grated Cheddar cheese
8 oz. softened cream cheese
1/2 med. onion, minced
2 T. dried chives, or 3 T. fresh, chopped fine
2 T. mayonnaise
1 c. nuts, well chopped

Mix together all ingredients, except the nuts, and form a ball. Roll in the nuts until evenly coated. Chill until serving time.
Served with crackers or garlic toast, this recipe is perfect for holiday parties. It's pretty when rolled in 1/2 cup fresh parsley mixed with the nuts.

From: American Profile

Party Meat Balls

1 (11 1/8 oz.) can Campbell's condensed Italian tomato soup
1 lb. ground beef
1/4 c. dry bread crumbs
1 egg, beaten
1 T. Worcestershire sauce
1/2 c. water
2 T. vinegar
2 tsp. packed brown sugar

Mix 1/4 cup soup, beef, bread crumbs, egg and Worcestershire sauce thoroughly. Shape firmly into balls (1/2-inch). Arrange in shallow-sided baking pan. Bake at 350° for 15 minutes, or more, until meat balls are done. Yield: 48 meat balls.
In saucepan, mix remaining soup, water, vinegar and sugar. Over medium heat, heat to boiling. Cover and cook over low heat 5 minutes. Add meat balls. Heat through.
Can keep hot in crock-pot.

From: Campbell's Back Label Recipes

Party Pretzels*

2 (15 oz.) pkg. pretzels
1 pkg. Good Seasons Italian dressing
1 btl. popcorn oil
1 tsp. garlic powder
1 tsp. garlic salt

Mix in large roaster. Mix last 4 ingredients and pour over pretzels. Mix well every 20 minutes for 2 hours. <u>No bake</u>!
Freezes well.

LaVonne Zinck

Peanut Sauce

2 garlic cloves
2 T. dark soy sauce
1/4 c. smooth peanut butter
1 T. sugar
1 c. water
2 sm. fresh, red hot chilies, seeded (I have used dried red chilies)

Crush garlic into a small saucepan with the soy sauce, peanut butter, sugar and water. Cut the chilies in small slivers and add to the saucepan. Bring to a simmer, then simmer 5 minutes, stirring constantly. If sauce is very thin, simply simmer until slightly thickened. Remove from heat; cool to room temperature before serving. If sauce solidifies upon cooling, thin it with a little hot water.

Serve with crisp raw vegetables, such as carrots, celery, cucumbers, green beans, small whole radishes, cauliflowers (blanched, if desired) and edible-pod peas.

Marlene Clemens via Kim Kusler

Pepper Pots*

Red, green and yellow peppers   Chip dips of your choice

Cut tops off peppers. Remove seeds. Fill with dips or spreads for crackers or raw vegetables.
Very colorful on appetizer tray.

Christine Daggett via Janice Diemert

Pizza on a Bun*

Combine:
1/4 c. oil
1 lb. Cheddar cheese, grated
1 sm. can tomato sauce
1 sm. can black olives, chopped
1 sm. can mushrooms, chopped
1 med. onion, chopped
1 tsp. oregano

Spread on bun halves and broil.

Nadine Olson

Pizza Sandwich

1 lb. ground beef, raw
1 tsp. oregano
Salt & pepper, to taste
2 T. chopped green onions
1 sm. can ripe olives, chopped
3 T. grated Parmesan cheese
1 can tomato paste

Mix all together. Divide 1 French bread loaf in half; spread mix on both sides (both halves). Top with sliced tomatoes. Put in 375° oven for 20 minutes. Top with American cheese, sliced diagonally. Put back in oven for 5 minutes, until cheese melts.

From: Claire Ann Shover Nursery School, Fergus Falls, MN

Quick Bar-B-Que Sauce*

Equal parts of ketchup & Coke,
   plus brown sugar, to taste

Pour over browned hamburger, ribs, etc.

Tammy Buhr Erickson

Red Pepper Cheese Ball*

2 (8 oz.) pkg. cream cheese
1 (3 oz.) pkg. thinly-sliced chopped beef (I used Buddig brand)
1 T. lemon juice
2 T. Miracle Whip
1/2 c. chopped fresh sweet red bell peppers
6 green onions, chopped (the white & green top)

Mix cream cheese until fluffy. Add rest of ingredients. Stir together by hand. Shape into a ball. May roll into a log and press in chopped walnuts or pecans. Chill. Serve with favorite crackers or fresh vegetables.

Colleen Clancy

Refried Bean Dip

1 can refried beans
1 (8 oz.) ctn. sour cream
1 (12 oz.) jar salsa
1 (8 oz.) pkg. Cheddar cheese, shredded
1/2 c. black olives, cut in circles
1 bag tortilla chips or crackers

Spread beans on bottom of 8x8-inch pan. Add the sour cream, salsa, cheese and black olives. Let stand or set, covered, for 8 hours to blend flavors. Eat with tortilla chips or crackers.

Darlene Trader

Rhubarb Slush

12 c. rhubarb, cut up
9 c. water
2 c. sugar
1 (6 oz.) can frozen lemonade
1 (3 oz.) box raspberry Jello
1 qt. 7-Up

Simmer rhubarb and water for 1/2 hour. Run through a sieve. Discard pulp. Reheat and add sugar, lemonade and Jello until all is dissolved. Freeze. To serve, mix 2/3 cup slush to 1/3 cup 7-Up.

Andrea Richman

Reuben Hot Dip*

8 oz. Swiss cheese, shredded
8 oz. cream cheese
3 pkg. corned beef
1 c. sour cream
15 oz. sauerkraut

Melt all together. Serve with crackers (especially good with Triscuits). Keep hot in a small crock-pot.

Joan Holland

Salmon Dip

1 (15 oz.) can salmon
1 (8 oz.) pkg. cream cheese, softened
1/3 sm. onion, chopped
1 T. lemon juice
1/2 tsp. prepared horseradish
1/4 tsp. liquid smoke
Salt, to taste

Remove bones and skin from salmon. Mix with rest of the ingredients. Refrigerate until ready to eat. Serve with crackers. Yield: 1 1/2 cups.

This dish is best if allowed to chill for at least a few hours in the refrigerator to blend the flavors. A few chives make a complimentary garnish.

From: American Profile

Only fools live in the past or carry envy to the present.
Chi Chi Rodriguez

Seven Wives Inn Granola

8 c. regular oatmeal (not quick)
1 c. brown sugar
1 1/2 c. wheat germ
8 oz. coconut (wide, unsweetened)
8 oz. sliced almonds
8 oz. cashews
3 oz. sunflower seeds
1/2 c. water
1/2 c. oil
1/2 c. honey
1/2 c. peanut butter
2 tsp. vanilla

Mix the first 7 "dry" ingredients in a large bowl. Mix well and bring to a boil the next 5 "wet" ingredients. Add wet to dry. Blend well. Spread on 2 large cookie sheets. Bake about 2 hours in a 200° oven, until coconut becomes brown around the edges. Add 1 cup raisins after baking, if desired. Yield: about 5 pounds.

*From: 50 Years at the Lord's Table,
St. Luke's Lutheran,
La Mesa, CA*

Simply Surprising Dip*

8 oz. cream cheese, softened
1/2 (12 oz.) btl. chili sauce
1/4 c. chopped green onions
1/4 c. chopped green bell pepper

Spread cream cheese in 10x10-inch dish or pie plate. Top with chili sauce. Sprinkle with green onions and green pepper. Chill for 1 hour. Serve with bite-sized tortilla chips. Yield: 16 servings.

Marlene Almlie

Shrimp Dip Deluxe*

1 (8 oz.) pkg. soft Philadelphia cream cheese
1 sm. jar cocktail sauce
1 (6 oz.) can shrimp, drained

Note: Keep these 3 ingredients on hand for quick hors d'oeuvres.

On a colorful or crystal plate, spread the cream cheese. In center, cover with 1 small jar cocktail sauce. Top with can of drained shrimp. Cover with Saran Wrap and chill. Before serving, sprinkle with your favorite spice. Add some fresh parsley sprigs around edge of plate.

Easy party snack with Wheat Thins.

Ann Richman Cease

Skinny Vegetable Dip*

2 T. milk
1 (12 oz.) ctn. cottage cheese
  (consider using nonfat)
1/4 c. salad dressing (consider using light or no-fat)
1/4 tsp. garlic powder
1 tsp. onion salt
Dash of cayenne pepper

Blend until smooth using a blender, mixer or food processor. Don't tell anyone that his dip is actually good for them.

Carolyn Jorrisen,
Times Record

Snack Mix*

1 to 2 (6 oz.) pkg. Bugles
1 box Crispix
1 bag tiny pretzels (not sticks)
1 bag oyster crackers
1 box Cheese Nips
1 tsp. onion powder
1 T. garlic salt
1 btl. Orville Redenbacher popcorn oil
1 can mixed nuts
1 box white Cheddar crackers

Pour all into large turkey roasting bag and add oil; shake well. Put in freezer bag as this freezes well.

Juanita Beilke

Snowmints

Wash hands. In a bowl, mix together 1 tablespoon softened butter (do not use margarine), 1 tablespoon light corn syrup, 1/8 teaspoon salt and 1/2 teaspoon mint extract with a fork. Gradually add 1 cup powdered sugar. When dough becomes too stiff to stir, knead with hands. Make 12 snowmen with 3/4 of dough by forming 2 or 3 marble-size balls for each one. Stack balls on waxed paper to make bodies. Divide rest of dough in half. Knead 1 drop blue food coloring into one half. Wash hands. Knead 1 drop red and 2 drops yellow food coloring into other half. Wash hands. For each snowman, press on candy sprinkles for mouth, eyes and buttons. Form a scarf, hat or earmuffs, and nose out of colored dough. Press features in place. Store in refrigerator.

These melt-in-your-mouth mints will tickle your tastebuds!

Ann and Allison Cease

Snowman Soup*

Cocoa mix (as many packages as you have guests, Swiss Miss with marshmallows is a good choice)

Chocolate Kisses
Candy canes, for stirring

Add hot water to each package of cocoa mix. Drop in chocolate Kiss and more marshmallows, if desired. Stir with candy cane.
Sip slowly and relax!

Colleen Clancy

Stuffed Mushrooms*

2 ctn. whole mushrooms
1 lb. sausage

8 oz. cream cheese

Preheat oven to 350°. Wash mushrooms well and remove stems for chopping. Brown sausage and chopped stems in skillet. Mix in cream cheese until melted. Place mushroom shells on baking sheet and fill with sausage/cheese mixture. Bake for 25 minutes.

Ann Cease,
From: Northern Lights magazine

Sugar and Spice Snacks

1 (6 oz.) pkg. Bugle corn snacks
2 c. mixed nuts
2 T. orange juice or water
2 egg whites

1 1/3 c. sugar
2 tsp. ground cinnamon
1 tsp. ground allspice
1/2 tsp. ground ginger

Heat oven to 275°. Grease jellyroll pan. Mix Bugles and nuts in large bowl. Beat orange juice or water and egg whites in small bowl with wire whisk or hand beater until foamy. Mix in remaining ingredients. Stir into Bugles and nut mixture until well coated. Spread in pan. Bake for 45 to 50 minutes, stirring every 15 minutes, until light brown and crisp. Cool and store in airtight container.

From: Times Record – Prairie Fare,
Julie Garden-Robinson

Strawberry Freezer Jam*

3 c. crushed strawberries   5 c. sugar

Mix and let stand for 20 minutes, stirring once in awhile. Take 1 cup water and 1 package Sure-Jell; boil for 1 minute. Add to berries while still hot. Stir in 2 minutes. Put in jars and let set. Stir in jars to prevent settling. Put on covers and into freezer.

LaVira Eggermont

Summertime Fruit Slush

3 c. water
3 c. sugar
1 (15 1/2 oz.) can crushed pineapple
6 bananas, cubed
1 (10 oz.) jar maraschino cherries
1 (12 oz.) can frozen orange juice
1 (12 oz.) can water

In a large pan, boil water and sugar for 10 minutes. Add pineapple, bananas and cherries. Set aside and cool. In another bowl, mix orange juice and water. Place in freezer and chill, but do not freeze. Remove and mix in fruit mixture. Freeze. When ready to serve, partially thaw. Yield: about 2 quarts.

If you prefer a less sweet drink, use 1 cup sugar and 1 cup honey instead of 3 cups of sugar. Save a few maraschino cherries for garnish. Skewer fresh pineapple, bananas and cherries for a complimentary garnish.

Marie Monforte

Tex-Mex Dip*

1 (11 1/4 oz.) can Campbell's condensed fiesta chili beef soup
1/3 c. Open Pit original flavor barbecue sauce
2 T. finely-chopped green pepper
1 T. finely-chopped onion
Sour cream
Tortilla chips

In saucepan, mix soup, barbecue sauce, pepper and onion. Over medium heat, heat through, stirring often. Top with sour cream. Serve with tortilla chips for dipping. If desired, garnish with fresh chives and chili peppers. Yield: 1 1/2 cups.

Preparation time: 10 minutes. Cook time: 5 minutes.

From: Campbell's Back Label Recipes

Texas Trash

3 c. Golden Graham cereal
1 c. pretzels
1 c. cashews
1 c. pecan halves
1 (12 oz.) pkg. white chocolate chips

Melt white chocolate chips. Pour over cereal, pretzels and nuts in a large bowl. Mix until all ingredients are coated. Line a cookie sheet with waxed paper. Spread mixture on cookie sheet. Let cool overnight. Break up and store in covered container in refrigerator if you won't be using all at one time.

Karen Tabor

Toffee*

1/2 lb. butter
1 c. brown sugar

Cook 2 ingredients in heavy pot, stirring constantly, for 8 minutes. Pour into buttered 8-inch pan. Cool slightly. Place plain Hershey bars on top. Let melt. Spread, then sprinkle on chopped nuts.

*From: Clair Ann Shover Nursery School,
Fergus Falls, MN*

Tropical Fruit Dip/Fruit Butter*

Fruit and mustard give a surprise taste wake-up.

1/3 c. honey mustard
1/3 c. light mayonnaise
1 1/2 tsp. brown sugar
1 1/2 tsp. grated lime peel

Combine all ingredients; mix well. Use as a dipping sauce for your choice of fruit, which might include banana, strawberries, pineapple mango or melon. Yield: 2/3 cup sauce.

FRUIT BUTTER:
1/2 c. butter, softened
3 T. honey mustard
2 T. orange marmalade

Blend all ingredients until smooth. Spoon into a ramekin. Serve as a spread with croissants or on toasted bread, muffins or pound cake. Yield: about 1/2 cup spread.

From: Associated Press – The Fargo Forum

Sangria

1 btl. juicy red wine
1 orange
1 lime
1/2 lemon
3 T. orange liqueur
1 to 2 T. sugar
Ice cubes
6 oz. ginger ale

Pour the wine into a large pitcher. Wash the orange, lime and lemon. Cut them into thin slices and add to the pitcher. Add the orange liqueur and sugar. Marinate for a few hours in the refrigerator. (The sangria will taste better if you leave it overnight.)

When ready to serve, fill the pitcher with ice cubes, add the ginger ale and stir well. Serve with a wooden spoon in the pitcher.

Tips: According to wine maven Joshua Wesson, wines for sangria should be young, inexpensive, juicy and fruity. Wines aged in wood should NOT be used, e.g. zinfandel, cabernet sauvignon, merlot and chardonnay.

Joshua Wesson,
Deb Grovum, Ann Cease

Summer Slush*

1 lg. can pineapple juice
2 cans frozen lemonade
1 can lemon juice
3 pkg. powdered raspberry punch
4 c. sugar, or to taste
1 pkg. frozen raspberries

Add water to make 2 gallons in a Giant Canister and freeze.

From: Tupperware

Sweet Pickles from Dill Pickles

1 (46 oz.) jar dill pickles   1 1/2 c. white sugar (or less)

Drain juice from 46-ounce jar of dill pickles. Discard juice. Cut pickles into 1-inch cubes; return to jar. Add 1 1/2 cups white sugar to pickles in jar (use less sugar, if desired). Seal jar. Turn and shake until sugar is dissolved. Let jar stand for a few minutes between shakes. Place pickle jar in refrigerator.

Pickles will become crisp as they stand in refrigerator. Excellent!

Melva Glemming

Tortilla Roll-Ups*

4 oz. cream cheese
8 oz. sour cream
1 sm. can chopped green chilies
1 sm. can chopped black olives
1 c. shredded Cheddar cheese
1/2 c. chopped onion, or to taste
1 pkg. dry ranch dressing

Mix well. Spread on soft tortillas. Roll up, chill, slice.
Note: Drain green chilies and black olives well – too much liquid will keep them from staying together.

Marcy Rynestad

Triscuit Nachos*

Triscuit crackers (Original)
Salsa (your favorite, or Taco Bell thick & chunky)
Kraft shredded 4-Cheese Mexican-style cheese

Place crackers, topped with salsa and cheese on a microwave plate. Microwave on HIGH for 15 to 20 seconds, until cheese is melted. Serve with your favorite toppings: sour cream, sliced ripe olives, chopped jalapeño peppers.
3 crackers = 1 serving.

From: Triscuit box

Turkey Taco Dip*

1 lb. ground turkey
1 sm. jar salsa
Taco seasoning mix
1 c. refried beans
1 pkg. Velveeta Mexican-style cheese

Brown turkey; stir in taco mix and salsa. Remove from heat. In a casserole dish, layer refried beans, turkey mixture and cheese. Make 3 layers, ending with cheese. Bake until hot, approximately 20 to 25 minutes, at 350°. Top with sour cream, chopped lettuce and chopped tomato, if desired.

Jennifer Perry

Veggie Sandwich*

1 slice pumpernickel bread, toasted
1/2 c. zucchini, grated
2 thin green pepper slices
2 thin tomato slices
2 T. grated carrots
2 or 3 sliced fresh mushrooms
1 oz. Cheddar cheese
1 oz. Swiss or Monterey Jack cheese

Place all raw vegetables on toasted bread. Top with cheese. Broil until cheese is bubbly. Yield: 1 serving.

Debbie Tuck

Water Chestnuts in Bacon and Sauce*

1 can water chestnuts
1 lb. bacon, cut in half crosswise

Wrap half of bacon slice around each chestnut. Secure with toothpicks. Bake at 350° in large cake pan for 30 minutes. Pour off grease (this can be done ahead of time, then frozen, if desired).
Make a sauce of 3/4 cup ketchup and 1/2 cup sugar. Mix stir and heat. Drizzle over chestnuts. Reheat for 30 minutes. Serve hot.

Gayla Glemming Satre

White Italian Sangria

4 to 6 fresh peaches
4 to 6 T. orange liqueur
1 lime
1 lemon
1 orange
1/2 c. brandy
1 btl. dry white wine
1/4 c. sugar
2 T. fresh lemon juice
2 c. club soda or ginger ale

Peel the peaches and prick them all over with the tines of a fork. Marinate them in the orange liqueur for a minimum of 4 hours – overnight if possible – in a tightly-covered container in the refrigerator. Turn the peaches a few times to coat them all over. (The peaches may turn slightly brown during this step.) Slice the lime, lemon and orange into thin slices and place the slices in a 3-to 4-quart glass pitcher. Add the brandy, wine and sugar; stir well. Let the mixture stand at room temperature for about 1 hour.
When ready to serve, add the lemon juice and peaches, with their liquid, and club soda or ginger ale. Stir the mixture well. Add ice cubes to tall glasses and pour mixture over.
When orange liqueur is called for, any of these will do: Grand Marnier, Triple Sec or Curacao.

From: Star Tribune, July 10, 1980

White Sangria

1 btl. fruity white wine
1 pear
1 Granny Smith apple
1 lime
1/2 lemon

3 T. orange liqueur
1 to 2 T. sugar
Ice cubes
6 oz. ginger ale

Pour the wine into a large glass pitcher. Wash the pear, apple, lime and lemon. Cut them into thin slices and add to the pitcher. Add the orange liqueur and the sugar. Marinate for a few hours in the refrigerator. (The sangria will taste better if you leave it overnight.)

When ready to serve, fill the pitcher with ice cubes, add the ginger ale and stir well. Serve with wooden spoon in the pitcher.

Joshua Wessom,
Debbie Grovum, Ann Cease

Where wine goes in, wit goes out.

Notes & Recipes

Brake for Breads & Brunch

From a kitchen plaque in the home of
Florence Cease:

Yew tak yust ten big potatoes
Den yew boil dem til dar don,
Yew add to dis some sweet cream
And by cups it measures vun.

Den yew steal 'tree ounces of butter
And vit two fingers pench some salt,
Yew heat dis very lightly
If it ain't gude it is your fault.

Den yew roll dis tin vit flour
And light brown on stove yew bake.
Now call in all Scandihuvians
Tew try da fine lefse yew make!

Brake for Breads & Brunch

Almond-Poppy Seed Bread

3 c. flour
1 1/2 c. milk
2 1/2 c. sugar
1/2 tsp. salt
1 1/2 tsp. baking powder
1 1/2 tsp. almond flavoring
1 1/2 tsp. butter flavoring
1/2 tsp. vanilla
3 eggs
2 T. poppy seeds
1 c. + 2 T. oil

Mix all ingredients together in a bowl. Pour into 2 loaf pans or 1 bundt pan. Bake at 325° for 1 hour to 1 hour and 15 minutes (or until toothpick inserted in center comes out clean).

Kim Kusler

Apple Oatmeal Breakfast Cookies*

1 1/2 c. uncooked quick rolled oats
1/4 c. whole wheat flour
1/2 c. chopped dates
1/2 tsp. salt
1/4 c. chopped walnuts
1/4 c. orange juice
1 1/2 c. shredded apple

Preheat oven to 375°. Combine oats, flour, salt, walnuts, orange juice and shredded apple. Let stand 10 minutes. Drop by large tablespoons 2 inches apart onto cookie sheets, sprayed with cooking spray. Bake for 18 to 22 minutes, until light brown. Yield: 2 1/2 dozen cookies.

From: The Fifty Best Oatmeal Cookies in the World, p. 40

Home should be more than a filling station.

Apple-Sausage French Toast
Plan ahead…start the night before.

3/4 lb. bulk pork sausage
2 med. apples, peeled & cut into 1/4" slices
6 eggs
2 1/2 c. milk

1/3 c. maple syrup
1/2 tsp. ground nutmeg
18 slices French bread (1/2" thick)

In a skillet, cook sausage over medium heat until no longer pink; drain. Remove and set aside. Add apples to the skillet; cover and cook for 3 to 5 minutes, or until tender, stirring occasionally.

In a bowl, lightly whisk the eggs, milk, syrup and nutmeg until combined. In a greased 9x13x2-inch baking dish, arrange half of the bread. Top with the sausage, apples and remaining bread. Pour egg mixture over the top. Cover and refrigerate for 8 hours or overnight.

Remove from the refrigerator 30 minutes before baking. Bake, uncovered, at 350° for 45 to 50 minutes, or until eggs are set and bread is golden. Yield: 9 servings.

From: Taste of Home magazine

Bacon 'N' Egg Tacos*

6 eggs
1/4 c. crumbled, cooked bacon
2 T. butter or margarine
3 slices process American cheese, diced

1/4 tsp. salt
1/4 tsp. pepper
6 (6") flour tortillas, warmed
Salsa (opt.)

In a bowl, beat the eggs. Add bacon. Melt butter in skillet over medium heat. Add egg mixture; cook and stir until the eggs are completely set. Stir in the cheese, salt and pepper. Spoon 1/4 cup down the center of each tortilla; fold sides over filling. Serve with salsa, if desired. Yield: 6 servings.

One egg for each taco, so recipe can be divided to serve a few, or doubled to serve a crowd.

From: Taste of Home magazine

Baked Cinnamon Bread Custard*

14 slices cinnamon bread, 1/2" thick
6 eggs
3 egg yolks
1 c. sugar
3 c. milk
2 c. half & half
1 tsp. vanilla
Powdered sugar

Arrange bread in a double layer in a lightly-greased 9x13-inch baking pan. (Cut bread as needed to cover bottom of pan.) Whisk together eggs, egg yolks and sugar. Gradually add milk, half & half and vanilla. Pour mixture over bread. Bake in a 375° oven for 25 to 30 minutes, or until a knife inserted in the center comes out clean. Dust with powdered sugar while warm and serve.

A tablespoon of orange zest whisked into the egg mixture adds a nice flavor twist. This dish would be ideal for a midnight breakfast.

Joann Parker,
From: American Profile

Blueberry French Toast

12 slices day-old white bread, crusts removed
2 (8 oz.) pkg. cream cheese
1 c. fresh or frozen blueberries
12 eggs
2 c. milk
1/3 c. maple syrup

SAUCE:
1 c. sugar
2 T. cornstarch
1 c. water
1 c. fresh or frozen blueberries
1 T. lemon juice
1 T. butter or margarine

Cut bread into 1-inch cubes, place half in greased 9x13-inch baking dish. Cut cream cheese into 1-inch cubes; place over bread. Top with blueberries and remaining bread. In large bowl, beat eggs. Add milk and syrup. Mix well. Pour over bread mixture. Cover. Chill 8 hours or overnight. Remove from refrigerator 30 minutes before baking. Cover and bake at 350° for 30 minutes. Uncover; bake 25 to 30 minutes more, until golden brown and center set. Yield: 6 to 8 (or more) servings.

Sauce: In saucepan, combine sugar and cornstarch. Add water. Boil over medium heat 3 minutes, stirring constantly. Add blueberries, reduce heat and simmer 8 to 10 minutes, until berries burst. Remove from heat, add lemon juice and butter. Stir until melted. Serve over French toast. Yield: 1 3/4 cups.

Delicious served with side dish of smoked sausage for contrast.
I had compliments on this fairly easy company breakfast.

Sonny Spitzer

Breakfast in a Glass*

3/4 c. cold pineapple juice
1 sm. ripe banana, cut in chunks
5 strawberries, sliced (can use frozen)
1/4 c. nonfat plain yogurt
1 T. honey (opt.)

Place all ingredients in a blender and process to the desired consistency. Yield: 1 serving.

From: Fargo Forum

Breakfast Fritters*

1/2 ripe banana, mashed
1 egg
1/2 tsp. sugar
Dash of salt
1 slice bread, crumbled

Beat first 4 ingredients until frothy. Stir in crumbled bread and beat until frothy again. Spray frypan with nonstick cooking spray. Brown on both sides. Serve with margarine.
Variation: Omit banana. Cook fritter, then top with 1/2 cup warmed applesauce and cinnamon.

Ann Cease via Debbie Tuck

Breakfast Casserole*

6 slices buttered bread
7 eggs
6 slices American cheese
6 slices bread, cubed
2 c. diced ham or cooked sausage
2 1/2 c. milk
1 stick margarine

Place buttered bread, buttered-side down, in a 9x13-inch pan. Place slices of cheese on top of bread. Distribute the meat evenly over cheese. Mix eggs and milk; pour over the top. Place cubed bread over entire casserole. Melt margarine and pour over top of bread. Refrigerate for a few hours or overnight. Bake, uncovered, for 1 hour at 350°.

From: North Central School Cookbook

Breakfast Pizza*

1 lb. sausage	5 eggs
1 pkg. crescent rolls	1/2 c. milk
1 c. frozen hash browns, thawed	1/2 tsp. salt
	1/8 tsp. pepper
1 c. sharp Cheddar cheese, shredded	2 T. grated Parmesan cheese

Cook sausage; drain off fat. Separate crescent rolls. Place ungreased pizza pan with points toward center. Press over bottom and up sides to form crust. Seal edges. Spoon sausage over crust. Sprinkle with hash browns. Top with Cheddar cheese.

In bowl, beat eggs, milk, salt and pepper. Pour over crust. Sprinkle with Parmesan cheese. Bake at 375° for 25 to 30 minutes. Yield: 8 to 10 servings.

From: Best of the Best from the Great Plains

Breakfast Soufflé*

1 1/2 lb. sausage	1 1/2 tsp. dry mustard
9 eggs	3 slices white bread, cut into 4" cubes
3 c. milk	
1 tsp. salt	1 1/2 c. grated Cheddar cheese

Brown sausage. Drain and cool. Stir together beaten eggs, milk, bread, mustard, salt, cheese and sausage. Pour into a 9x13-inch greased casserole dish. Bake, uncovered, in a 350° oven for 1 hour. Yield: 12 servings.

Variations: Grated Swiss or Mozzarella cheese can be substituted for Cheddar. Green onions, sliced olives or chopped fresh parsley are colorful and flavorful additions to this recipe.

Bette K. Tumiati,
From: American Profile

Brunch Cheesecake*

2 tubes crescent rolls	1 egg
2 (8 oz.) pkg. cream cheese, softened	3/4 c. sugar
	Cinnamon/sugar

Heat oven to 350°. Press 1 tube crescent rolls on bottom of 9x13-inch pan. Mix cheese, egg and sugar together well. Spread over crescent rolls in pan. Top with second tube crescent rolls. Spread out over cheese mixture. Top with cinnamon and sugar. Bake for 30 minutes at 350°.

Best served warm – good cold also.

Colleen Clancy

Buttermilk Nut Bread*

1 egg
1 c. packed brown sugar
2 T. shortening, melted
2 c. all-purpose flour
3/4 tsp. baking powder
1/2 tsp. baking soda
1/2 tsp. salt
1 c. buttermilk
1/2 c. chopped nuts

In a mixing bowl, beat the egg. Gradually beat in brown sugar and shortening. Combine flour, baking powder, baking soda and salt; add to egg mixture alternately with buttermilk. Beat just until moistened. Stir in nuts. Pour into a greased 5x9x3-inch loaf pan. Bake at 350° for 45 to 55 minutes, or until a toothpick inserted near the center comes out clean. Cool for 10 minutes; remove from pan to a wire rack. Yield: 1 loaf.
Sue Ross,

Casa Grande, AZ
From: Quick Cooking magazine

Cheddar Biscuits*

2 c. all-purpose flour
2 tsp. baking powder
1 tsp. baking soda
1/2 tsp. salt
3/4 c. shredded Cheddar cheese
1/3 c. shortening
1 c. buttermilk

In a bowl, combine flour, baking powder, baking soda and salt. Cut in cheese and shortening until crumbly. Add buttermilk; stir just until moistened. Turn onto a lightly-floured surface; knead 8 to 10 times. Roll out to 1/2-inch thickness. Cut with a 2 1/2-inch biscuit cutter. Place on an ungreased baking sheet. Bake at 425° for 10 to 12 minutes, or until golden brown. Yield: 16 biscuits.
Serve warm with eggs and bacon.
Biscuits freeze well, too.

Colleen Horudko,
From: Quick Cooking magazine

In youth we learn, in age we understand.
Marie Ebner Eshenbach

Cherry Cream Crescents*

1 (8 oz.) pkg. cream cheese, softened
1 c. confectioners' sugar
1 egg, separated
2 (8 oz.) tubes refrigerated crescent rolls
1 (21 oz.) can cherry pie filling

In a mixing bowl, beat cream cheese, sugar and egg yolk. Separate dough into 16 triangles; place on lightly-greased baking sheets. Spread 1 tablespoon of cream cheese mixture near the edge of the short side of each triangle. Top with 1 tablespoon pie filling. Fold long point of triangle over filling and tuck under dough. Lightly beat egg white; brush over rolls. Bake at 350° for 15 to 20 minutes, or until golden brown. Yield: 16 rolls.

Elouise Bullion,
From: Quick Cooking magazine

Chocolate Banana Bread

1/2 c. butter
1 c. sugar
2 eggs
1 1/2 c. flour
2 T. cocoa
1 tsp. baking soda
1 tsp. salt
1/2 tsp. cinnamon
1/2 c. sour cream
1 tsp. vanilla

Cream butter and sugar. Add eggs, one at a time, beating well. Mix flour and cocoa. Add remaining dry ingredients and then add dry mixture to creamed mixture. Add sour cream and vanilla; mix well. Spoon batter into 2 bread loaf pans lightly sprayed with Pam. Bake at 350° for 55 minutes. Cool 10 minutes in pans before removing loaves. Then cool on wire racks.

Irma Swanke,
From: Season's Eatings in ND

Cinnamon Pastries*

2 pkg. refrigerator biscuits
1/4 c. sugar
1 tsp. cinnamon

Preheat Fry Baby or deep-fryer. Drop biscuits into oil, they raise and fry in seconds, when brown on one side, flip over. Brown that side. Place on paper towel for a few seconds to drain. Place in sugar/ cinnamon mixture and shake until covered. Serve while still warm. Yield: 16 pastries.
   Time: 15 to 20 minutes or less.
   Best served when warm. They fry very fast.

Brenda O'Brien

Cocoa Muffins*

These muffins have an intense chocolate flavor that should satisfy almost any craving. If you need even more chocolate, you can add some chocolate chips to the batter. But beware, they will add quite a bit more fat to the recipe.

In one mixing bowl, combine:
1/2 c. flour
1/2 c. cocoa powder
1/2 tsp. baking soda
1/2 tsp. baking powder

In a second bowl, combine:
1/2 c. puréed pumpkin
1/2 c. honey
1 tsp. vanilla
3 egg whites

Add the liquid ingredients to the dry ingredients and mix thoroughly. Spoon into muffin cups and bake at 350° for 18 to 20 minutes, or until they spring back when touched lightly.

Charlie Trottier,
From: Mayo Clinic Women's Health Letter

Cottage Cheese Scrambled Eggs*

6 eggs
3/4 c. cottage cheese
2 T. milk
1 T. chopped chives
1/2 tsp. salt
1/8 tsp. pepper
2 T. butter

Beat eggs. Stir in cottage cheese, milk, chives, salt and pepper. Melt butter over low heat. Add egg mixture. Turn with spatula as it begins to thicken. Do not overcook. Serve immediately.

Cream Bread*

Thaw a loaf of Rhodes frozen bread, flatten in a greased cake pan. Mix:
1 c. cream
1 c. white (or brown) sugar
1 tsp. vanilla

Pour over bread. Let rise until light, 2 hours or so. Bake at 350° for 20 to 25 minutes, until done.

Marion Gerntholz

Dole Pineapple Berry Smoothie*

Combine 1 (20-ounce) can Dole crushed pineapple in juice, undrained, 1 cup Dannon plain nonfat yogurt, 1 Dole banana, 1 cup Dole pineapple juice, 1/2 cup fresh or frozen strawberries or raspberries and 1/2 cup ice cubes in blender or food processor. Cover; blend until smooth. Yield: 4 (8-ounce) servings.

From: Magazine Ad

Dutch Babies*

1 T. butter or margarine
1/2 c. flour
1/2 c. milk
1 tsp. vanilla
3 eggs

Preheat oven to 450°. Melt butter or margarine in pie dish that Dutch babies will be cooked in. Watch carefully, as soon as butter is melted, roll pan slightly to coat sides. Mix flour, milk, vanilla and eggs until smooth. Pour into the pie pan. Bake for 15 minutes. Top with applesauce, syrup or cheese. Yield: 2 servings.

Janice Lee

Easy Cornbread (or Muffins)*
(From the Quaker Oats Company)

1 1/4 c. flour
3/4 c. cornmeal
1/4 c. sugar
2 tsp. baking powder
1/2 tsp. salt (opt.)
1 c. skim milk
1/4 c. vegetable oil
2 egg whites or 1 egg, beaten

Heat oven to 400°. Combine dry ingredients. Stir in milk, oil and egg, mixing just until dry ingredients are moistened. Pour batter into 12 greased or paper-lined medium muffin cups. Bake for 15 to 20 minutes, until golden brown.

Eat them while they are hot and fresh with a bit of jam or honey.

Carolyn Jorissen

Egg Sausage Soufflé

1 (6 oz.) box seasoned croutons (4 c.)
2 c. Cheddar cheese
24 oz. sm. link pork sausage
4 eggs
2 1/2 c. milk
1 tsp. dry mustard
1 can cream of mushroom soup
1/2 can milk, measured

Brown sausage; drain, and cut into bite-size pieces. Spray or grease a 9x13-inch pan. Spread croutons; top with cheese and sausage. Beat eggs with milk and mustard; pour over crouton mix. Cover and refrigerate overnight. Before baking dilute soup with 1/2 can milk. Pour over casserole. Bake at 325°, uncovered, for 90 minutes. Remove from oven and cover with foil lightly and let set 10 minutes before serving.

Note: Can use bacon or ham or omit meat.

Lyndi Dittmer-Perry

Friendship Bread

1 c. vegetable oil
1 1/2 c. sugar
1 tsp. vanilla extract
3 lg. eggs
1/2 tsp. salt
2 tsp. cinnamon
2 1/2 c. flour
1 1/4 c. milk
1/2 tsp. baking soda
1 (3.4 oz.) box instant vanilla pudding
1 1/2 tsp. baking powder
1/3 c. chopped black walnuts (opt.)

Preheat oven to 325°. Combine oil, sugar, vanilla, eggs, salt and cinnamon in a large bowl. Add flour, milk, baking soda, pudding, baking powder and walnuts, if desired. Mix well. Grease two large loaf pans and sprinkle with a mixture of sugar and cinnamon. Pour in bread mixture and sprinkle any leftover sugar mixture on top. Bake for 1 hour.

This moist breast is even better with a bit of icing drizzled over the top.

Jim Evans,
From: American Profile

Fruit Fizz*

1 sm. watermelon
1 med. green apple
1 (15 oz.) can fruit cocktail, drained (reserve syrup)
1 (12 oz.) can or btl. Sprite or 7-Up, chill until ready to use

Slice watermelon and apples. Remove seeds of melon and core of apple. Cut into tidbits or squares. Soak apples in fruit cocktail syrup for 10 minutes. Drain. Combine with watermelon and fruit cocktail. Chill. Pour well-chilled Sprite or 7-Up over just before serving. Yield: 10 servings.

Joy Jasmann

Jiffy Cinnamon Rolls*

4 to 5 c. all-purpose flour, divided
1 (9 oz.) box one-layer white cake mix
2 (1/4 oz.) pkg. quick-rise yeast
1 tsp. salt
2 c. warm water (120° to 130°)
2 T. butter or margarine
1/2 c. sugar
1 T. cinnamon

In a large mixing bowl, combine 3 cups flour, cake mix, yeast, salt and warm water; mix until smooth. Add enough remaining flour to form a soft dough. Turn out onto a lightly-floured surface; knead until smooth, about 6 to 8 minutes. Roll dough into a 9x18-inch rectangle. Spread with butter and sprinkle with sugar and cinnamon. Roll dough, jellyroll-style, starting with the long end. Slice the roll into 1-inch circles. Place on greased cookie sheets. Cover, let rise in a warm place until doubled, about 15 minutes. Bake at 350° for 15 to 18 minutes. Frost, if desired. Yield: 18 rolls.

LaVira Eggermont

Good manners is the awareness of other people's feelings...if you have awareness, you have good manners and it doesn't matter which fork you use.
Emily Post

Healthy Apple-Walnut Muffins*

Made with no added fat or sugar, these tasty muffins use fruit and buttermilk to keep them moist.

2 c. all-purpose flour
1 tsp. baking soda
1/4 tsp. ground cinnamon
1/4 tsp. ground ginger
1/4 tsp. ground allspice
1/4 tsp. ground nutmeg
1/4 rounded tsp. salt
2 lg. eggs

1 c. + 2 T. frozen, thawed apple juice concentrate
2/3 c. buttermilk
2 T. oat bran
2 sm. Granny Smith apples, peeled, cored & chopped
1/2 c. chopped walnuts (about 1 1/3 oz.)

GARNISH:

1 sm. Granny Smith apple, peeled, cored & cut into 12 thin slices

Preheat oven to 375°. Grease 12 standard-size muffin pan cups or line with paper liners. Mix together flour, baking soda, cinnamon, ginger, allspice, nutmeg and salt. Mix together eggs, apple juice and buttermilk. Stir flour mixture and oat bran into egg mixture until dry ingredients are just moistened. Do not overmix. Gently stir in chopped apples and nuts. Spoon batter into prepared pan, filling cups two-thirds full. Garnish each muffin with an apple slice. Bake muffins until lightly golden and tops spring back when pressed, 25 minutes. Transfer pan to a wire rack to cool slightly. Turn muffins out onto rack to cool completely. Yield: 12 muffins.

Preparation time: 15 minutes. Baking time: 25 minutes.

Baking Tips: Instead of frozen apple juice concentrate, use other bottled fruit juice concentrates. Health food stores generally carry the best variety. Experiment with such interesting flavors as papaya, pineapple and mango for a tropical taste.

From: Great American Home Baking

Hot Curried Fruit*

1 can chunk pineapple
1 can apricots
1 can peaches

1/4 c. brown sugar
1/2 tsp. curry powder
2 T. butter

Drain fruit and arrange in 1 1/2-quart baking dish. Sprinkle fruit with mixture of sugar, curry powder and butter. Bake at 350° for about 20 minutes.

A good dish for brunch.

Nadine Olson

Italian Bread*

1 loaf Italian bread, sliced
(but not through)

Spread with mixture of:
1 stick butter, whipped
2 tsp. chives
1/2 tsp. lemon pepper
1/2 tsp. poppy seeds
1/2 T. mustard

Spread on both sides of slices, put a slice of Swiss cheese between each slice, also bacon bits. Wrap loaf in foil. Bake at 350° for 15 to 20 minutes, uncover and bake 10 to 15 minutes longer.

Nadine Olson

Jamaican Banana Bread

2 T. softened butter or margarine
2 T. softened 1/3 less (fat) cream cheese
1 c. sugar
1 egg
2 c. flour
2 tsp. baking powder
1/2 tsp. baking soda
1/8 tsp. salt
1 c. mashed bananas
1/2 c. skim milk
2 T. dark rum or 1/4 tsp. rum extract with 2 T. water
1/2 tsp. grated lime rind
2 tsp. lime juice
1 tsp. vanilla
1/4 c. chopped pecans
1/4 c. flaked coconut

TOPPING:
Spoon on after bread is baked:
1/4 c. brown sugar
2 tsp. butter
2 tsp. lime juice
2 tsp. rum
2 T. chopped pecans
2 T. flaked coconut

Preheat oven to 375°. Beat butter and cream cheese. Add sugar and egg. In separate bowl, combine flour with dry ingredients. Then combine bananas, milk and flavorings in another bowl. Add to sugar mixture, alternating with dry mixture, beginning and ending with flour. Stir in pecans and coconut. Bake for 55 to 60 minutes in 4x8-inch loaf pan. Cool slightly on wire rack.

Topping: Combine brown sugar, butter, lime juice and rum in saucepan and simmer; cook 1 minute, stirring constantly. Remove from heat. Add nuts and coconut. Spoon over the bread.

Delicious! Taken from Cooking Lite, so healthy as well.

Doris Sauerland

Jiffy Cornbread Bake*

1 lb. hamburger, lean

Brown in pan sprayed with Pam. Add 1 1/2 cup thick salsa. Mix together. Add 1 cup canned corn, drained. Place meat and salsa, corn in 7x11-inch casserole, sprayed with Pam.
Mix cornmeal muffins as directed. Pour over hamburger mix in pan. Bake at 400° for 15 to 20 minutes, until top is done.

From: Radio Talk Show

Lazy Man's Rolls*

12 frozen dinner rolls
1/2 c. packed brown sugar
1/2 tsp. (or more) cinnamon
1/2 c. melted butter

Arrange frozen rolls in bundt pan sprayed with nonstick cooking spray. Blend brown sugar and cinnamon with melted butter in bowl. Pour over rolls. Let rise at room temperature overnight. Bake at 350° for 20 to 25 minutes, or until golden brown. Invert onto serving plate. Yield: 12 servings.

Cheryl Rostad

Maple Breakfast Rolls*

1/4 c. butter or margarine, melted
1 c. packed brown sugar
1/2 c. chopped walnuts
1/3 c. maple syrup
1 (8 oz.) pkg. cream cheese, softened
1/2 c. confectioners' sugar
4 (6 oz.) tubes refrigerated buttermilk biscuits

In a small bowl, combine the butter, brown sugar, nuts and syrup. Spread into a greased 9x13x2-inch baking dish; set aside. In a small mixing bowl, beat the cream cheese and confectioners' sugar until smooth.
On a lightly-floured surface, roll out each biscuit into 4-inch circle. Spread 1 tablespoon of cream cheese mixture down the center of each biscuit. Bring dough from opposite sides over filling just until edges meet; pinch to seal. Place seam-side down over nut mixture. Bake at 350° for 25 to 30 minutes, or until golden brown. Immediately invert onto a serving plate. Serve warm. Yield: 8 to 10 servings.

Nadine Brissey,
From: Taste of Home magazine

Never-Fail Buns

3 c. warm water
1/2 c. sugar
2 pkg. dry yeast
2 tsp. salt

Mix above ingredients. When yeast float to the top (about 5 minutes), add 4 beaten eggs and 1/2 cup soft margarine. Beat with electric mixer. Add 10 to 12 cups flour until dough is not sticky. Knead and let rise 1 1/2 hours in a warm place. Knead down, let rest 15 minutes. Form into buns. Let rise. Bake for 20 minutes at 350°. Yield: 5 dozen.

LaVira Eggermont

No-Knead Dark Bread

2 1/2 c. warm water
2 pkg. dry yeast
1 T. salt
1/4 c. oil
4 T. honey, brown sugar or molasses
2 c. white flour
1 c. whole wheat or rye flour

Combine above ingredients in large mixing bowl; mix with electric mixer, then add to mix by hand 2 cups white flour and 1 cup whole wheat or rye flour. Let rise in covered bowl 1/2 hour. Stir the batter down and pour into 2 greased bread pans. Let rise until 1/4-inch from top of pan, about 40 minutes. Bake at 375° for 45 to 50 minutes.

Claudia Richman Nelson

Nutmeg Sour Cream Muffins*

1 egg
1 c. (8 oz.) sour cream
1/2 c. + 1 tsp. sugar, divided
2 T. shortening
1 1/3 c. all-purpose flour
1 tsp. baking powder
1/2 tsp. baking soda
1/2 tsp. salt
1/2 tsp. ground nutmeg

In a mixing bowl, beat egg until light and fluffy. Add sour cream, 1/2 cup sugar and shortening; beat well. Combine the flour, baking powder, baking soda and salt; stir into sour cream mixture just until moistened. Fill greased or paper-lined muffin cups 3/4 full. Combine nutmeg and remaining sugar; sprinkle over muffins. Bake at 400° for 15 minutes.

A speedy accompaniment to a salad lunch. A sprinkling of sugar and nutmeg creates the tempting topping.

Pat Walter,
From: Quick Cooking magazine

Oatmeal Rolls

1 c. oatmeal (1/2 c. each quick & old-fashioned)
3 T. soft margarine
2 c. boiling water
2 pkg. yeast, dissolved in 1/3 c. warm water with 1 tsp. sugar
2/3 c. brown sugar, packed
1 T. white sugar
1 1/2 tsp. salt
5 c. all-purpose flour

In a large bowl, pour the boiling water over the oats and margarine. Stir and cool to lukewarm. Add sugars, salt and dissolved yeast to oatmeal mixture. Knead in the flour, a cup at a time. Allow dough to rise in a warm place for 1 hour. Punch down. Form into rolls and place in greased 9x13-inch baking pan. Allow to rise again for 20 to 30 minutes. Bake in a 350° oven for 20 to 25 minutes, until golden brown.

This is an excellent basic recipe for cinnamon rolls. Roll the dough out 1-inch thick after the first rising. Sprinkle with cinnamon and brown sugar. Roll into a pinwheel and cut into 1 1/2-inch rolls. Bake and glaze with icing.

Carol Meyer,
From: American Profile

Success is more attitude than aptitude and never forget that failure is only the opportunity to begin again more intelligently.
(Anonymous)

Ole's Swedish Hot Cakes*

3/4 c. (1 1/2 sticks) butter
1 c. flour
1 tsp. baking powder
1 tsp. sugar
1/4 tsp. salt

1 1/2 c. milk
1/2 c. half & half
Grated zest of 1 orange
3 eggs, separated

Melt the butter and let it cool slightly. Meanwhile, stir together the flour, baking powder, sugar and salt in a mixing bowl. Whisk in the milk, half & half and zest. The mixture will be very liquid; don't worry. Whisk in egg yolks (this will thicken the batter slightly). In a separate bowl, beat the egg whites until soft peaks form and stir them gently into the batter. (You don't need to fold them; the batter is not that delicate.) This will thicken it to about the consistency of a good homemade eggnog. Whisk in the melted butter. (The recipe can be made ahead to this point and refrigerated, tightly covered, overnight.)

Heat a nonstick skillet over medium-high heat until drops of water skitter across the surface. Slowly pour one-half cup of the batter in the center, forming as much of the circle as you can (using a ladle of measuring cup with a lip makes this easier).

Cook until the bottom of the pancake has lightly browned and the top begins to look slightly dry, about 3 minutes. Flip the pancake and cook until it feels somewhat firm when pressed lightly in the center, 2 more minutes.

Remove from the pan and keep warm in the oven. Serve 2 pancakes per person. Yield: 4 servings.

Total time: 20 minutes.

QUICK STRAWBERRY SAUCE:
1/2 lb. strawberries, rinsed
   & hulled

1/4 c. sugar
1 T. orange juice

Place the strawberries, sugar and orange juice in the work bowl of a food processor and pulse 4 or 5 times just to chop them small. Don't purée. Transfer the mixture into a small nonstick skillet and cook over medium-high heat until it begins to thicken, about 5 minutes. Set aside until ready to use. Yield: 8 (1 cup) servings.

Total time: 10 minutes.

This recipe comes from the Little River Inn just south of town of Mendocino along the northern California coast. The pancakes can be served with maple syrup or a big spoonful of strawberry sauce in the center. To really gild the lily, you can top that with a spoonful of whipped cream. By Russ Parsons, Los Angeles Times.

From: AP – The Forum

One-Pan Applesauce-Raisin Coffeecake*

2 c. Bisquick
1 c. applesauce
1/2 c. white sugar
1/4 c. brown sugar
1/4 c. vegetable oil
1/2 tsp. cinnamon
1/2 tsp. nutmeg
1/8 tsp. cloves
2 eggs
1/2 c. chopped walnuts
1/2 c. raisins

STREUSEL TOPPING:
1/4 c. sugar
2 T. Bisquick
2 T. margarine
2 tsp. cinnamon

Grease and flour (or spray) a 9x13-inch pan. In the pan, mix all but the streusel topping ingredients together. Then, mix the streusel topping ingredients and sprinkle on top of cake batter. Bake at 350° for 35 to 40 minutes. Yield: 16 to 20 pieces.

Kim Kusler

Orange-Nut Bread

2 1/2 c. sugar
1 1/2 c. vegetable oil
6 eggs
1 1/2 c. milk
4 1/2 c. flour
3/8 tsp. salt
3 tsp. baking powder
Rind of 4 oranges, grated (1 c.)
2 c. chopped nuts (or as desired)

Mix by hand, in order given. Put in four 3 5/8 x 7 3/8 x 2 1/4-inch pans. Bake for 1 hour to 1 1/4 hours at 350°.
Mix the following and pour over loaves immediately after removing from pan:
Juice from the oranges (4)   1/4 c. sugar

Let stand in pan for at least 1 hour or until cool.

Betty Kappel

Orange Peach Smoothies*

2 c. frozen unsweetened
  peach slices, thawed
1 c. milk
1 (6 oz.) can frozen orange
  juice concentrate, thawed
1/4 tsp. almond extract
1 pt. vanilla ice cream
3 drops each red & yellow food
  coloring (opt.)

In a blender, combine the peaches, milk, orange juice concentrate and extract. Add ice cream; cover and process until smooth. Add food coloring if desired. Pour into glasses; serve immediately. Yield: 4 servings.

Orange Pull-Apart Bread*

1 (8 oz.) tube refrigerated
  crescent rolls
2 T. butter or margarine,
  softened
2 T. honey
1/2 to 1 tsp. grated orange peel

Open tube of crescent rolls, do not unroll. Place on a greased baking sheet, forming one large roll. Cut into 12 slices to within 1/8-inch of bottom, being careful not to cut all the way through. Fold down alternating slices from left to right to form a loaf. Bake at 375° for 20 to 25 minutes, or until golden brown. Combine butter, honey and orange peel; brush over the loaf. Serve warm. Yield: 6 servings.

Brushed with a sweet orange glaze, the bread is so popular I usually double or triple the recipe.

Kristin Salzman,
From: Quick Cooking magazine

Overnight Omelet

1 lb. sausage
5 eggs
1 (12 oz.) can evaporated milk
1 1/2 slices bread, torn
2 c. Cheddar cheese

Brown sausage and drain. Beat eggs and milk; add torn bread pieces, cheese and sausage. Pour into 9x13x2-inch baking dish. Cover with foil and refrigerate overnight. Bake at 350° for 40 minutes. Yield: 8 servings.
  Recipe from The Cinarron, Elkharn, Kansas.

From: Best of the Best from the Great Plains

Pecan Orange Muffins*

Finely grate peel from 1 orange. Finely chop 3/4 cup pecans. Beat 1 stick margarine and 1 cup sugar. Beat in 2 eggs, one at a time. Stir in grated peel. Add 1 teaspoon baking soda to 1 cup buttermilk. Fold in 1 cup flour with 1/2 the buttermilk, then fold in another cup flour and rest of buttermilk. Fold in pecans. Bake at 375° for 20 minutes, or less. Spoon orange juice over muffins and sprinkle with sugar. Let stand 5 minutes before removing from pan.

Nadine Olson

Pecan Pie Muffins*

1 c. light brown sugar
1/2 c. all-purpose flour
2 eggs
2/3 c. melted butter (I use salted butter)
1 c. chopped pecans

Preheat oven to 350°. Mix all ingredients in a bowl with a wooden spoon. Pour into a greased miniature muffin pan, filling each cup 2/3-full. Bake for 12 to 15 minutes. Yield: 2 1/2 to 3 dozen.
Garnish each muffin with a pecan half.

Carolyn Hays,
From: American Profile

You don't need to practice every day...only the days that you eat.
Sin'ichi Suzuki, answering a student's question.

Pumpkin Maple Cream Cheese Muffins*

CREAM CHEESE FILLING:
4 oz. cream cheese, softened
2 T. packed brown sugar
1 1/2 tsp. maple flavoring

MUFFINS:
2 c. all-purpose flour
3/4 c. packed brown sugar
1/2 c. chopped walnuts
2 tsp. baking powder
1 tsp. ground cinnamon
1/2 tsp. baking soda
1/4 tsp. salt
2 eggs
1 c. Libby's solid pack pumpkin
3/4 c. Carnation evaporated milk
1/4 c. vegetable oil
2 tsp. maple flavoring

NUT TOPPING:
Combine in small bowl:
2 T. packed brown sugar
1/4 c. chopped walnuts

Preheat oven to 400°. Combine flour, sugar, nuts, baking powder, cinnamon, baking soda and salt in large bowl. Mix eggs, pumpkin, evaporated milk, oil and maple flavoring in medium bowl. Add second mixture to dry ingredients. Blend. Into 12 paper-lined cupcake tins, spoon 1 heaping teaspoon of cream cheese mix into middle of batter mix. Batter should make 12 muffins. Sprinkle nut mix over top. Bake in 400° oven on middle shelf, 20 minutes, or until muffins test done (insert toothpick). Cool in pan 5 minutes. Serve warm.

Marcella Richman,
From: Libby's solid pack pumpkin label

Quiche I*

1/2 c. butter
10 eggs
1/2 c. flour
1 T. baking powder
2 (8 oz.) cans green chilies
1 pt. cottage cheese
1 lb. Monterey Jack cheese, grated
Garlic salt, to taste

Beat eggs and mix with all ingredients. Pour into 9x13x2-inch pan. Bake at 400° for 15 minutes. Reduce to 350° and bake for 35 to 40 minutes longer. Can be mixed night before.

From: 50 Years at the Lord's Table,
St. Luke's Lutheran Church,
La Mesa, CA

Quiche II*

Pie crust mix for 9" pie crust
2 T. butter or margarine, melted
1/2 (10 oz.) pkg. frozen, chopped broccoli, thawed & well drained
2 oz. Swiss cheese, shredded (1/2 c.)
1/2 c. sliced, cooked ham
2 eggs
1/2 c. heavy or whipping cream
1/4 tsp. salt

Prepare pie crust mix as label directs. Roll out and place in pie pan. Brush melted butter over bottom of pastry. Set aside. Preheat oven to 375°. In small bowl, stir broccoli, Swiss cheese and ham until well mixed. Spoon into pie crust. In same small bowl, with wire whisk or fork, beat eggs, cream and salt until well blended. Spoon egg mixture over broccoli mix. Bake for 40 minutes, or until knife inserted in center of quiche comes out clean.

From: 50 Years at the Lord's Table,
St. Luke's Lutheran Church,
La Mesa, CA

Rich Pumpkin Coffeecake

2 (16 oz.) pkg. pound cake mix
4 tsp. pumpkin pie spice
2 tsp. baking soda
2/3 c. water
1 3/4 c. Libby's 100% natural solid pack pumpkin (15 or 16 oz. can)
4 eggs
Streusel Topping (recipe follows)

Combine pound cake mixes, pumpkin pie spice and baking soda in large mixer bowl. Add water, pumpkin and eggs; beat on medium speed for 3 minutes. Spread half of batter into greased 9x13-inch baking pan; sprinkle with half of Streusel Topping. Carefully spread with remaining batter; sprinkle with remaining Streusel Topping. Bake in preheated 325° oven for 50 to 55 minutes, or until wooden pick inserted in center comes out clean. Yield: 18 servings.

Streusel Topping: Combine 3/4 cup packed brown sugar, 3/4 cup chopped nuts and 1/2 cup all-purpose flour in medium bowl. Cut in 1/3 cup butter or margarine with pastry blender or two knives until crumbly.

From: Libby's pumpkin label

Scandinavian Cinnamon Rolls or Coffeecakes

Scald and cool:
1 c. milk

Mix in a large bowl:
1 c. flour   1/4 c. sugar
1 tsp. salt

Cut into flour:
1 c. butter or margarine

Mix:
1 pkg. regular yeast in 1/4 c. warm water, let rise a little while

Beat 3 egg yolks.
Pour cooled milk, egg yolks and dissolved yeast into flour/butter mixture. Mix and beat well. Cover and put in refrigerator overnight.

In morning, do either of the following: 1) Roll out half of dough. Spread with butter, cinnamon and sugar. Cut into 1-inch slices and put into greased muffin tins. Let rise 45 to 60 minutes. Bake at 375° for 20 to 25 minutes. Yield: about 2 dozen.

Or: 2) Roll out half of dough into a 11x14-inch rectangle on a greased cookie sheet. Recipe makes 2 of these (10 to 12 servings each). Mix together 4 ounce cream cheese, 2 to 3 tablespoons sugar and 1 tablespoon butter and 1 teaspoon lemon juice; spread on middle 1/3 of the sheet of dough. Next spoon 1/4 cup jam or marmalade onto the cream cheese mixture. (Or you can use a combination of brown sugar, butter, cinnamon and chopped nuts for the filling.)

Next cut 1-inch strips down each side of the uncovered dough. Alternately cross strips over the top of the filling, making a "braid" effect. Be sure to seal the ends of the strip well, to contain the filling. Let rise 45 minutes. Bake at 375° for 25 to 30 minutes. Drizzle with a vanilla powdered sugar icing. Cut into slices to serve.

Nancy King

Secret to Southern Cornbread*

Any good Southern cook will tell you that there are two secrets to perfect cornbread – good southern cornmeal and cast-iron.

Cornbread experts at Martha White, the makers of Martha White cornmeal and cornbread mixes, describe perfect cornbread as crispy and brown on the outside, moist and tender on the inside.

Good southern cornbread needs no adornment other than a pat of butter. But, for variety, the Martha White kitchen suggests easy additions you can stir into its famous Southern Cornbread recipe before baking. Create your own variation by combing any of the following suggestions:

1/2 c. cooked & crumbled bacon or fresh pork sausage
1 c. corn kernels
1/3 c. chopped green onion, bell pepper or green chilies
1/2 c. shredded Cheddar cheese
1/3 c. chopped fresh parsley
2 tsp. chili powder or rubbed sage
1/2 tsp. coarsely-cracked black pepper

SOUTHERN CORNBREAD:
1 egg
1 1/3 c. milk or 1 3/4 c. buttermilk
1/4 c. vegetable oil or melted shortening
2 c. Martha White self-rising cornmeal mix

Heat oven to 450°. Grease muffin cups or corn stick molds and place in oven to heat. Prepare batter as directed above. Pour into prepared pans. Bake at 450° for 15 to 20 minutes, or until golden brown. Yield: about 1/2 medium muffins or 16 corn sticks.

From: Times Record, Valley City

Simply Coffeecake*

1 1/2 c. flour
1 c. sugar
1 tsp. baking powder
1/2 tsp. salt

3 T. butter
1 egg
3 peeled apples, chopped

CRUNCH TOPPING:
1/4 tsp. brown sugar
1/2 c. chopped pecans
1 tsp. cinnamon

Mix together; sprinkle over cake batter.

Preheat oven to 350°. Mix and toss first 7 ingredients. Put in square (9-inch) baking pan (sprayed with Pam). Top with crunch topping. Bake at 350° for 45 to 50 minutes on middle shelf. (Check with toothpick – don't overbake.)

As heard on the radio

Sourdough Biscuits*

2 pkg. yeast, dissolved in
1 c. warm water

Then add:
2/3 c. sugar
3/4 c. oil
4 c. buttermilk

Blend well and add:
4 c. flour

Mix again, then add:
4 1/2 c. flour
4 tsp. salt
8 tsp. baking powder
1 tsp. baking soda

Mix well; ready to bake. Pinch off balls of dough, or may be rolled out and cut. Bake for 20 minutes at 375°.
Use Fix-N-Mix to store balance of dough in refrigerator.

From: Old Tupperware recipe

Stormy Day Breakfast Bread Pudding

2 c. low-fat milk
2 eggs
1/3 c. packed brown sugar
3/4 tsp. vanilla extract
1/4 tsp. salt
4 c. dry bread cubes
1 (16 oz.) can pear halves or slices, drained, chopped
1/8 tsp. ground cinnamon
1 c. low-fat granola

Preheat oven to 350°. Lightly grease an 8x8-inch pan. In large bowl, combine milk, eggs, brown sugar, vanilla and salt; add bread cubes. Pour mixture into prepared pan. Arrange pears over bread; sprinkle with cinnamon, top with granola. Bake at 350° for 50 to 60 minutes, or until knife inserted in center comes out clean. Let set for 5 minutes. Serve warm. Yield: 6 servings.

The name of this comfort-food-style breakfast dish suggests its bad weather season appeal; use of canned fruit means it's easy to prepare any season.

*From: The Forum,
Fargo, ND*

Super Quick Sticky Caramel Rolls*

1/4 c. margarine or butter, melted
1/4 c. brown sugar
1 T. corn syrup
1/4 c. pecans
1 (11 oz.) can soft refrigerated breadsticks
1 T. sugar
1/2 tsp. cinnamon

Heat oven to 375°. In a small bowl, combine margarine, brown sugar and corn syrup. Blend well. Spread evenly in the bottom of an 8- or 9-inch round pan, ungreased. Sprinkle with pecans. Remove dough from can. Separate into 8 coils. <u>Do not unroll breadsticks!</u> In a shallow dish, combine sugar and cinnamon. Dip one cut side of each coil in this mixture. Arrange coils sugared-side down over pecans in pan. Sprinkle with any remaining sugar mixture. Bake at 375° for 19 to 24 minutes, or until golden brown. Cool 1 minute. Invert onto serving plate. Serve warm. Yield: 8 rolls.

Janet Maesse,
From: Recipes and Remembrances,
Ulen, MN

Swiss Onion Loaf*

1 c. (4 oz.) shredded Swiss cheese
2 T. dried minced onion
1 pkg. hot roll mix
1 T. butter or margarine, melted

In bowl, combine cheese and minced onion with dry ingredients of hot roll mix. Prepare mix according to package directions. Turn onto a floured surface, knead until smooth and elastic, about 6 to 8 minutes. Shape into a 5-inch ball and place on a greased baking sheet. Cover and let rise in a warm place for 30 minutes, or until doubled. Bake at 375° for 25 to 30 minutes, until golden brown. Brush with butter. Remove to a wire rack to cool. Yield: 1 loaf.

Marlys Freadhoff

Tex-Mex Biscuits*

2 c. biscuit/baking mix
2/3 c. milk
1 c. (4 oz.) finely-shredded
   Cheddar cheese
1 (4 oz.) can chopped green
   chilies, drained

In a bowl, combine biscuit mix and milk until a soft dough forms. Stir in cheese and chilies. Turn onto a floured surface; knead 10 times. Roll out to 1/2-inch thickness; cut with a 2 1/2-inch biscuit cutter. Place on an ungreased baking sheet. Bake at 450° for 8 to 10 minutes, or until golden brown. Serve warm. Yield: about 1 dozen.

From: Quick Cooking magazine

Tinnicci's Coffeecake

1/4 c. sugar
1/4 c. pecan pieces
1 tsp. cinnamon
1 tsp. cocoa
1 box white cake mix

1 sm. box instant pudding mix,
   vanilla
2 eggs, beaten
8 oz. sour cream
3/4 c. milk
1/4 c. oil

GLAZE FROSTING:
1 c. powdered sugar

1/2 tsp. vanilla
1 1/2 T. milk

In small bowl, mix sugar, pecans, cinnamon and cocoa. Set aside. In larger bowl, mix cake mix, instant pudding, eggs, sour cream, milk and oil. Beat until smooth. Pour 1/2 batter into greased and floured fluted tube pan (bundt pan). Sprinkle nut mixture in and follow with remaining batter. Bake at 325° for 55 to 60 minutes. Cool 10 to 15 minutes, then remove from pan. Continue to let cool and glaze, if desired.

Jim Perry

Tortillas and Eggs*

This comes together real fast. The trick is to throw the tortillas in the pan to cook first, then chop, grate and mix.

Corn tortillas
Extra-virgin olive oil
Eggs
Milk
Grated sharp Cheddar cheese
5 finely-chopped green onions
Finely-chopped cilantro
Sliced avocado
Salsa or hot sauce*

*The absolute best is Tuong Ot Sparacha hot chili sauce (Huy Fong Foods, Inc.), a Vietnamese hot sauce form Rosemeed, CA – **www.huyfong.com** - 626-286-8328.

Cut corn tortillas into 1-inch squares (3 tortillas for 2 eggs and one more for each additional egg). Put them in pan with light oil at medium heat, cook until lightly browned and crisp. Beat the eggs with a dash of milk, toss into pan with browned tortillas. Stir in chopped green onions and a small handful of cheese. Put cooked tortillas and eggs on plate, place sliced avocado over the cooked tortillas and eggs. Sprinkle cilantro over all of it. Drizzle salsa or hot sauce on top and serve.   *Tom Lopez*

Travis' Mexican Omelette*

Chorizo or a spicy sausage
1/4 c. green onion, sliced
1 c. sliced fresh mushrooms
1 tomato, chopped
4 eggs, beaten
1/4 c. milk
Salt & pepper, to taste
1 c. Cheddar cheese, shredded
Sour cream
Salsa

Sauté sausage, onion, mushrooms and tomato. Add eggs, milk, salt and pepper; scramble. Fold in the cheese. Serve topped with sour cream and salsa.   *From: Best of the Best from the Great Plains*

Yellow Bread*

1 pkg. yellow cake mix
1 pkg. instant lemon pudding
3/4 c. vegetable oil
3/4 c. water
4 eggs
1 tsp. vanilla

Beat together for 8 minutes at high speed. Put 1/2 of batter in 2 loaf pans. Mix 1/4 cup sugar and 1 teaspoon cinnamon; pour over batter in loaf pans. Run knife through batter to marbleize. Pour remaining batter over this. Bake at 325° to 350° for 45 to 60 minutes.

I have also used white cake mix and pistachio pudding. This is very good, too.   *Lynette Lehfeldt*

Zucchini Oatmeal Muffins*

1 1/4 c. sugar
3/4 c. oil
4 eggs
1 T. baking powder
1 tsp. salt
1 tsp. cinnamon
2 1/2 c. flour
1/2 c. quick oatmeal
1 1/2 c. shredded zucchini

Cream together sugar and oil. Add eggs. Add baking powder, salt, cinnamon, flour and oatmeal. Stir in zucchini. Bake in muffin tins at 400° for 18 to 23 minutes.

From: Heitkamp Family recipes

Zucchini Pancakes*

2 c. zucchini, unpeeled & shredded
1/3 c. Bisquick baking mix
1 tsp. parsley
1/4 c. Parmesan cheese, grated
1/8 tsp. pepper
1/8 tsp. salt
1 egg
1 tsp. dry onion

Mix together and fry in shortening until golden brown.

Doris Goberville,
From: Swanke Reunion Cookbook '90

The world is a stage and most of us are desperately under-rehearsed.

Notes & Recipes

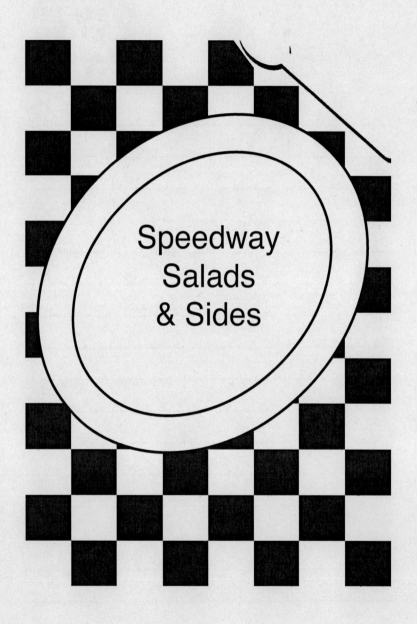

Speedway Salads & Sides

Notes & Recipes

Speedway Salads & Sides

Ada's Black Cherry Jello

2 (3 oz.) pkg. black cherry Jello

2 cans black cherries, pitted

Prepare per package mix with Jello. Chill until set.

TOPPING:
1 (8 oz.) pkg. cream cheese

1 c. Cool Whip

Blend cream cheese and Cool Whip. Whip up until soft and fluffy, for spreading.

1 c. finely-chopped walnuts

Mix Jello and cherries. Put in 8x8-inch Pyrex pan and cool until set. Spread cream cheese topping over top. Sprinkle walnuts over top of cream cheese. Chill overnight and cut into squares.

This is the best with black cherry Jello and pitted black cherries. The red cherries do not taste right.

Patty Sather

Almond-Orange Salad

1/2 head lettuce, torn
3 green onions, sliced
1/3 c. caramelized almonds

1 (11 oz.) can drained mandarin oranges, or peel & slice fresh oranges

DRESSING: Mix well.
1/2 c. oil
2 T. sugar
2 T. cider vinegar

2 drops Tabasco sauce
4 tsp. salt
Dash of pepper

Layer caramelized almonds in a medium-sized bowl.

To caramelize the almonds, place the sliced almonds with 2 tablespoons white sugar in an ungreased skillet over medium heat. Stir almonds and sugar until crystallized.

Mmmmmm good!

Joyce Peterson

Apricot Salad*

1 (20 oz.) can crushed pineapple & juice
2 sm. pkg. apricot Jello
2 c. buttermilk
1 (12 oz.) ctn. whipped topping

Heat pineapple to boiling; stir in Jello. Let cool to room temperature. Fold in buttermilk and whipped topping. Blend well. Refrigerate.

Melva Glemming

Avocado Egg Salad

4 hard-cooked eggs, chopped
4 slices bacon, crisp-cooked, drained & crumbled
1 T. finely-chopped green onion
2 lg. avocados, halved & seeded
2 tsp. lemon juice
2 T. mayonnaise or salad dressing
1 tsp. prepared mustard
1/2 tsp. salt
Dash of pepper
Lettuce

In a small mixing bowl, combine eggs, bacon and onion. Carefully scoop out avocado halves, leaving firm shells; brush shells with a little lemon juice to prevent browning. Mash avocado pulp in mixing bowl. Stir together the mayonnaise, 2 teaspoons lemon juice, mustard, salt and pepper. Add mashed avocado and the egg mixture; spoon into avocado shells. Place filled avocados on lettuce-lined serving plates. Garnish with bacon curls. Yield: 2 servings.

Note: Can also be used as a filling in a popover.

Fair Hills & Wildflower Golf Resort

Avocado-Tomato Salad*

1 T. red wine vinegar
2 tsp. Dijon-style mustard
1/2 tsp. salt
1/2 tsp. dried oregano leaves
1/2 tsp. lemon juice
1/4 tsp. white pepper
lettuce
1 clove garlic, minced or pressed
1 1/2 tsp. olive oil or salad oil
3 med. tomatoes
1 lg. avocado
Butter lettuce or other soft leaf

In a small bowl, mix vinegar, mustard, salt, oregano, lemon juice, pepper and garlic. Using a fork. Gradually stir in olive oil or salad oil until well blended and slightly thick. Peel tomatoes and cut lengthwise in about 1/3-inch slices. Cut avocado in half, remove pit, peel and cut in about 1/3-inch slices. Lightly mix tomatoes, avocado slices and dressing. Yield: 4 servings.

Serve at once in lettuce-lined bowl or atop lettuce leaves on salad plate.

Fair Hills & Wildflower Golf Resort

Balkan Cucumber Salad

2 c. plain yogurt
1/2 garlic clove, crushed
1 T. white vinegar
1 1/2 tsp. salt
1 T. olive oil
1 T. chopped chives
1 tsp. chopped mint leaves, or 1/2 tsp. dried
1 1/2 c. peeled, seeded & diced cucumbers
1 c. seedless green grape halves

Place yogurt in a large bowl. Beat with an electric mixer until very smooth. Add garlic, vinegar, salt, olive oil, chives and mint leaves; beat 1/2 minute. Fold in cucumbers and grape halves. Refrigerate at least 1 hour before serving in salad bowls. Yield: 4 to 6 servings.

This easy and flavorful salad is a keeper. For color, add red and green grapes.

From: American Profile

Baked Cranberry Sauce

4 c. fresh cranberries, washed & dried
1 navel orange, washed, dried, halved, sliced & quartered
1 to 2 c. white sugar, depending on desired sweetness
1/3 c. brandy
1 c. pecans

Preheat oven to 300°. Lightly butter a 2-quart baking dish.

Combine cranberries and sugar in a bowl; toss to coat. Gently stir in apples and orange pieces. Toss and add pecans. Spoon mixture into prepared baking dish. Bake for 30 minutes. Remove and stir in brandy. Return to oven and bake for an additional 30 minutes, stirring often.

Serve in the baking dish, or transfer to a serving dish, individual orange shells or ramekins. May be served hot, at room temperature or chilled. Yield: 8 to 12 servings.

From: The Forum Food Section

Broccoli Peanut Salad*

2 lb. broccoli flowerets, washed & dried
1 1/2 c. honey-nut roasted peanuts
1 sm. btl. poppy seed dressing

Place broccoli, peanuts and dressing into plastic bowl with tight-fitting lid. Shake to distribute dressing. Serve immediately. Can also add green grapes.

Good salad to take to pot-lucks.

Carolyn Jolstad

Champagne Fruit Bowl*

1 qt. strawberries, halved
2 oranges, peeled & sectioned
2 kiwi, peeled & sliced
1 1/2 c. seedless red or green grapes
2 to 3 T. sugar
1 1/2 c. champagne

In a large bowl, combine fruit and sugar. Cover and chill until serving time. Just before serving, pour champagne over fruit. Serve with a slotted spoon. Yield: 8 to 10 servings.
Note: You may use 7-Up instead of champagne.

Esther Richman

Cherry Dessert or Salad

1 (21 oz.) can cherry pie filling
2 (3 oz.) pkg. cherry Jello
1 1/4 c. cream (10 oz.)
1 c. 7-Up (8 oz.)
1 c. water (8 oz.)

Mix 2 small packages of cherry Jello in 1 cup of near boiling water until thoroughly dissolved. Add cherry pie filling, 1 1/4 cups of cream, and 1 cup 7-Up. Mix well. Chill until set, 2 to 3 hours. Yield: 11 (5-ounce) servings.
Refrigerator shelf life up to 3 days.

Jacob Severson

Chicken-Rice Salad

2 c. cooked brown or wild rice
1 1/2 c. cooked, cubed chicken breast
1 c. green grapes, cut in half
1 c. red grapes, cut in half
3/4 c. slivered almonds
1 (5 1/2 oz.) can pineapple bits, drained
1 can mandarin oranges, drained

Cook juice of pineapple and oranges with 2 tablespoons cornstarch and 1 tablespoon sugar. Cook until thickened. Cool. Add grated rind of 1 orange (or, in a pinch, 2 to 3 tablespoons orange marmalade). Pour over first 7 ingredients. Refrigerate until serving time.

Marcella Richman

Coleslaw

1 med. head cabbage
2 or 3 stalks celery

DRESSING:
3/4 c. white sugar
1/2 c. oil
1/2 c. vinegar

1/2 green pepper
A little onion

1 tsp. salt
1/2 tsp. white pepper
2 tsp. celery seed
1 tsp. mustard seed

Cook dressing for 3 minutes. Cool and pour over cabbage mixture.

LaVira Eggermont

Cranberry Chutney

1/2 c. packed brown sugar
1/2 c. golden raisins
1 can whole cranberry sauce
1 (11 oz.) can mandarin oranges, drained
2 T. lemon juice

1/2 tsp. ground cloves
1/2 c. finely-chopped apples
1/2 c. finely-chopped celery
1/2 c. finely-chopped pecans or walnuts

Combine all ingredients in saucepan. Bring to a boil over medium heat, stirring to prevent sticking. Lower heat and simmer for 15 minutes, covered. Serve chilled.

Debbie Grieco

Cranberry Mold

1 pkg. sugar-free raspberry Jello
1 c. boiling water
1/2 c. cold water
2 tsp. fresh lemon juice
Dash of salt

1 c. canned whole cranberry sauce
1/2 c. in-own-juice crushed pineapple
1/2 c. finely-diced celery

Dissolve Jello and salt in boiling water. Add the cold water and lemon juice. Chill until slightly thickened. Drain the pineapple and fold the cranberry sauce, celery and pineapple into the Jello mixture. Chill until firm in an 8x8-inch pan, an oiled mold or individual molds. Garnish with mayonnaise. Yield: 8 servings.

For a larger group, use a large package of Jello, 1 can cranberry sauce and 1 can pineapple; double the other ingredients. Keeps well.

This salad is a must at Thanksgiving and Christmas in our house, according to our daughter, Judy Kalainov.

Marilyn Cunningham

Crunchy Coleslaw I

1/2 head cabbage
2 T. sunflower or sesame seeds, toasted
1/2 c. almonds, toasted
1/2 c. green onions, chopped
Chicken flavor Ramen noodles

DRESSING:
2 T. sugar
3 T. vinegar
1 tsp. salt
1/4 tsp. pepper
1/2 c. salad oil
1 chicken flavor pkt.

Roast seeds and almonds in oven. Mix together cabbage, nuts, onions and crumble uncooked noodles. Pour dressing over just before serving.

Joyce Harkins

Crunchy Coleslaw II*

1 (16 oz.) pkg. coleslaw mix
1 pkg. beef-flavored Ramen noodles
1/3 c. oil
1/2 tsp. garlic salt
Sliced almonds

Mix seasoning packet (from Ramen noodles) with garlic salt and oil. Break up noodles, add to slaw mixture just before serving. Top with almonds. Quick, easy and good! Got recipe from my sister-in-law, Janice.

Nancy Thiel

Deluxe Scalloped Corn*

1 stick margarine, melted
1 egg, beaten
1 c. sour cream
1 (16 oz.) can cream-style corn
1 (16 oz.) can whole kernel corn, do not drain
1 sm. box corn muffin mix

Preheat oven to 350°. Lightly grease a 7x11-inch baking pan. Combine melted margarine, egg, sour cream, cream-style corn and undrained whole kernel corn in a medium bowl; mix well. Add dry cornbread mix to the corn mixture and stir gently, just until mixed. Pour mixture into prepared baking dish. Bake 45 minutes.

Carol Sweeney,
Lyn Nichols

Easy Egg Salad*

3 hard-cooked eggs
3 T. mayonnaise
1 T. prepared mustard
1/8 T. salt
1/8 T. pepper
1/8 T. lemon juice
1 T. minced green onion

In a small bowl, combine mayonnaise, mustard, salt, pepper and lemon juice. Stir in eggs with a fork, chopping them into bite-sized pieces. Add green onion. Yield: 2 servings.
This tasty egg salad is especially good with fresh garden tomatoes. It's also great with alfalfa sprouts on a whole wheat bagel.

Nina Coomb

Fast Fruit Salad*

1 (20 oz.) can pineapple chunks
1 (16 oz.) can peach slices
1 (11 oz.) can mandarin oranges
3 bananas
2 chopped apples
1 pkg. vanilla instant pudding
1 1/2 c. milk
1/2 can (6 oz.) frozen orange juice
3/4 c. sour cream

Drain fruit and mix in bowl. Beat pudding mix, milk and orange juice. Beat in sour cream. Add to fruit. Chill.

From: NY Mills Cookbook (HS Band)

Festive Carrot-Apple Salad

2 to 3 c. grated carrots
3 c. diced apple, unpeeled
1/2 c. crushed pineapple
1/2 c. raisins, or red or green grapes
1 c. walnut or pecan pieces, or sunflower seeds
1 (8 oz.) ctn. pineapple yogurt

Mix ingredients together. Refrigerate. Can be made several hours before serving. Yield: 8 to 10 servings.
Variation: Lemon or vanilla yogurt makes a nice substitute if pineapple yogurt is hard to find.

Gretchen Knoll

Fudge-Stripe Salad*

Mix together:
- 2 c. buttermilk
- 2 pkg. instant vanilla pudding

Add:
- 1 (16 oz.) ctn. Cool Whip
- 1 sm. can crushed pineapple, well drained
- 1 sm. can mandarin oranges, well drained

Chill at least 2 hours, and just before serving, add 1/2 package crushed fudge stripe cookies. Don't crush the cookies too fine, larger pieces provide texture and crunchiness. Makes a big bowl.

LaVira Eggermont

Grape Chicken Salad*

- 2 c. grapes, halved
- 2 c. cooked, chopped chicken
- 1/2 c. chopped walnuts
- 1/3 c. celery slices
- 1/2 c. Kraft creamy cucumber dressing
- 1/4 tsp. ground ginger
- 4 cantaloupe wedges

Combine grapes, chicken, walnuts and celery. Add dressing and ginger, combined. Mix slightly. Chill.

For each serving, spoon over cantaloupe wedge. Garnish with additional grapes.

From: Herberger's Cookbook

Green Beans with Bacon

- 3 to 4 slices bacon, fried
- 2 c. or more green beans, drained

Drain bacon and crumble. Reserve bacon grease. Cook green beans, small amount of water in open-kettle to retain green color. Cook until tender when tested with fork. Drain beans. Pour bacon grease over beans. Heat until warm. Crumble bacon pieces over green beans.

Good for the taste buds – not for cholesterol.

Helen Fitzpatrick

Green Treasure Salad*

1 c. green apple, do not peel
1 c. green seedless grapes
1/2 c. mini marshmallows
1/2 c. lemon-flavored yogurt
2 T. slivered almonds

Dice apple and cut grapes in half. Mix together the apple pieces, grapes, marshmallows, yogurt and almonds. Yield: 4 (3/4-cup) servings.
Preparation time: 10 minutes.
Per Serving: Equals 1 fruit serving.
Variation: May substitute red grapes and red apples. If lemon yogurt isn't available use lime yogurt.
Recipe sponsored by the 5 Plus Barnes County Partnership.

Wanda Anderson

Grilled Chicken and Fruit Salad

4 boneless, skinless chicken breast halves
Barbecue sauce
1 (10 oz.) pkg. mixed salad greens
1 pt. raspberries
1/2 cantaloupe, peeled & cut into chunks
Ranch dressing

Place chicken on greased grill over medium-hot coals. Grill 10 minutes on each side, or until cooked through, turning and brushing occasionally with barbecue sauce. Cut into strips. Arrange greens and fruit on serving plate. Place chicken over greens. Serve with dressing. Yield: 4 to 6 servings.
Special Extra: Spread French bread slices with ranch dressing. Grill until lightly browned on both sides.

Health Salad

1 pkg. coleslaw greens (found in produce dept. in grocery store)
1 pkg. chicken Ramen noodles
1/2 c. unsalted sunflower seeds
1/2 c. slivered almonds
1/2 c. oil
3 green onions, chopped up
1 tsp. sugar (more if desired)
1 T. vinegar

Combine coleslaw greens and crushed Ramen noodles. Add almonds, seeds and onions. Mix chicken seasoning packet, oil, vinegar and sugar. Pour over coleslaw mixture. Serve immediately. Enjoy!

LaVira Eggermont

Honey-Mustard Dressing*

1/4 c. mayonnaise
1/4 c. Grey Poupon Dijon
  mustard
1/4 c. honey
1 T. regular mustard
1 T. vinegar
1/8 tsp. paprika

Mix all together. Shake well, or use a whisk to blend well.
I double this recipe. It is hard to buy good honey-mustard dressing, and found this recipe very good.

Diane Kohler

Hot Chicken Salad

2 1/4 c. cooked chicken, diced
2 c. chopped celery
1 T. chopped onion
1/2 c. slivered almonds
1 T. lemon juice
Dash of pepper
3/4 c. mayonnaise
1 1/2 c. shredded Cheddar
  cheese
1/2 c. crushed potato chips

Combine chicken, celery, onion, almonds, lemon juice, pepper and mayonnaise; mix lightly. Place in 8x8-inch baking dish. Spread cheese over mixture, then sprinkle the potato chips over the top. Bake in preheated 350° oven for 25 to 30 minutes. Yield: 6 servings.

Note: If you are in a hurry, this can be baked in the microwave in less time.

Virginia Maasjo

Lettuce-Fruit Salad*

Red leaf lettuce
1 mango or peach
1 pear
3/4 c. grapes (red, seedless)
Creamy poppy seed dressing

Tear cleaned lettuce into salad bowl (about 4 large leaves per person). Top with sliced mango, pear and grapes. This can also be divided into 4 or 5 individual bowls. Do not toss. Serve with a sweet dressing, such as poppy seed or raspberry. You can substitute canned or fresh pineapple, or strawberries for the pear. Yield: 4 or 5 servings.

I have used this for large groups by extending the amounts. A head of clean spinach can be used with or instead of lettuce.

Janice Diemert

Lettuce Salad

1/2 c. sliced almonds
1 T. + 1 tsp. sugar
1/2 sm. head lettuce, torn into bite-size pieces (3 c.)

SWEET AND SOUR DRESSING:
1/4 c. vegetable oil
2 T. sugar
2 T. white vinegar

2 med. stalks celery, chopped (1 c.)
2 T. thickly-sliced onions
1 (11 oz.) can mandarin oranges, drained

1 T. chopped fresh parsley
1/2 tsp. salt
Dash of pepper
Dash of red pepper sauce

Cook almonds and sugar in 1-quart saucepan over low heat, stirring constantly until sugar is melted and almonds are coated. Cool and break apart. Prepare Sweet and Sour Dressing.

Toss almonds, dressing and remaining ingredients.

May also use romaine lettuce, may leave pepper out. May substitute tarragon vinegar for the white vinegar. *Rosemary Johnson*

Lime Hershey Salad*

1 sm. pkg. lime Jello
1 c. boiling water
1/2 c. cold water

1 lg. Hershey bar (plain or almond)
1 c. whipping cream

Prepare Jello using hot and cold water. Let set in cake pan. When set, cut in cubes or shred. Chop Hershey bar and add to Jello. Whip cream and fold into Jello. Yield: 4 to 6 servings (can be doubled).

Pat Buerkle

Lime Salad*

1 (3 oz.) pkg. lime Jello
1/4 c. sugar
1 c. mini marshmallows
1 c. crushed pineapple, drained

1 c. whipping cream
1 (8 oz.) pkg. cream cheese
1/2 c. crushed nuts

Mix Jello, sugar and marshmallows in 1 cup boiling water, stir until marshmallows are melted. Add 1 cup cold water. Put in refrigerator until it starts to set. Add pineapple, cream cheese, whipped cream and nuts. Put in refrigerator to set. *Cathy Gubrud*

Mandarin Salad

1/2 c. sliced almonds
3 T. sugar
1/2 head iceberg lettuce
1/2 head romaine lettuce

DRESSING:
1/2 tsp. salt
Dash of pepper
1/4 c. vegetable oil

1 c. chopped celery
2 whole green onions, chopped
1 (11 oz.) can mandarin oranges, drained

1 T. chopped parsley
2 T. sugar
2 T. vinegar
Dash of Tabasco sauce

In a small pan over medium heat, cook almonds and sugar, stirring constantly until almonds are coated and sugar dissolved. Watch carefully as they will burn easily. Cool and store in airtight container.

Mix all dressing ingredients and chill.

Mix lettuces, celery and onions. Just before serving, add almonds and oranges. Toss with dressing. Yield: 4 to 6 servings.

Very good. Can also add chicken. *Doris Sauerland*

Melon Salad

2 limes + 2 tsp. lime peel zest
1/4 c. frozen orange juice concentrate
1/2 tsp. vanilla

1 cantaloupe
1 honeydew melon
2 c. seedless red grapes

Squeeze limes to get 6 tablespoons lime juice. Combine lime zest and juice with orange concentrate and vanilla. Cut melon in half, then cut each half in 1-inch wedges. Trim rind, cut into 3/4-inch pieces. Add grapes. Put in bowl. Pour dressing over; toss gently. Refrigerate until ready to serve. Yield: 8 servings. *Pampered Chef*

One cannot make soup out of beauty.
Swedish proverb

Old-time Fruit Salad

3 beaten eggs
3/4 c. sugar
3 T. butter, softened
1/2 c. lemon juice
3 Golden Delicious apples, peeled, cored & chopped
3 Red Delicious apples, peeled, cored & chopped
1 bunch seedless green grapes
1 bunch seedless red grapes
1 (20 oz.) can pineapple tidbits, drained
1/2 c. chopped pecans or walnuts
1 1/2 c. mini marshmallows

Combine eggs, sugar and butter in saucepan; stir in lemon juice. Cook over medium heat until thickened, stirring constantly. It will thicken quickly. Refrigerate until cool.

In a large serving bowl, place fruit, nuts and marshmallows. Pour dressing over mixture; mix well.

To retain the natural color of the apples, toss a little lemon juice in the bowl of apples and mix well before adding other ingredients. Yield: 8 servings.

Dora Lechman

Oven Orange-Glazed Carrots*

3/4 lb. baby carrots
3 T. dark brown sugar
3 T. butter
3 T. orange juice

Boil the carrots until just soft. Drain. Melt the butter in a saucepan. Stir in the brown sugar and orange juice. Toss in the cooked carrots. Place in a casserole dish, uncovered. Place in a preheated 375° oven. Bake (stirring frequently), until glazed (10 to 15 minutes). Serve warm.

Add whipped potatoes and baked ham to create a great Sunday dinner.

Poppy Seed Dressing*

1 1/2 c. sugar
2 tsp. salt
2 tsp. dry mustard
2/3 c. vinegar
3 T. onion juice
2 c. salad oil
3 T. poppy seeds

Wild Flower Golf Resort

Poppy Seed Dressing*

2 c. sugar
3/4 tsp. salt
3/4 tsp. onion powder
3/4 tsp. dry mustard
3/4 c. vinegar
1 c. vegetable oil
3/4 tsp. poppy seeds

Mix well.

Carolyn Jorrisen

Potato Pancakes for Two

2 med. potatoes
1 egg
2 T. all-purpose flour
1/2 tsp. salt
1/4 tsp. garlic salt
Cooking oil

Peel potatoes. Shred and rinse in cold water. Drain thoroughly; place in bowl. Add egg, flour, salt and garlic salt. Mix well.

In a skillet over medium heat, pour in about 1/4-inch of cooking oil. When heated, pour batter by 1/4 cupfuls into hot oil. Fry for 5 to 6 minutes on one side, then turn and fry other side for same amount of time. Fry until potatoes are tender and golden brown. Drain on paper towels. Yield: 2 servings.

Melva Glemming

Pizza Salad*

8 oz. cubed Mozzarella cheese
5 chopped tomatoes
3 chopped green peppers
4 oz. sliced pepperoni
1/4 c. chopped onion
1 (3 1/2 oz.) can sliced ripe
  or green olives

DRESSING:
1/3 c. tomato juice
1/4 c. vegetable oil
1/4 c. red wine vinegar
1/2 tsp. Italian seasoning

Combine.

From: Times Record

Quickie Chickie Salad*

2 c. cubed, cooked chicken (or turkey)
1 c. cut-up celery
1 c. red grapes, cut in half
1 c. green grapes, cut in half
1 sm. can pineapple chunks, drained
1 can mandarin oranges, drained

DRESSING:
1/2 c. mayonnaise
1/4 c. orange concentrate
1 T. honey mustard
1 T. balsamic vinegar

Marcella Richman

Fruit and Cookie Salad*

2 boxes coconut or banana cream instant pudding
2 c. buttermilk
12 oz. Cool Whip
2 (11 oz.) cans mandarin oranges, drained
1 (5 1/2 oz.) can crushed pineapple, drained
1 (1 lb.) bag fudge-stripe cookies (freeze in order to crush before use)

Mix first 5 ingredients. Crush the frozen cookies. Add 3/4 of cookie crumbs to salad mixture. Reserve 1/4 crumbs to sprinkle on top of salad. Refrigerate.

Bernita Landgrebe Voelker

Rose's Salad*
(Fast and Good)

2 (3 oz.) pkg. cherry Jello
2 c. boiling water

Dissolve Jello in water.
Add to Jello mix:
1 can cranberry sauce or gel

Cool.
Fold in:
2 c. sour cream

Refrigerate.

Nancy Thiel

Betty's Salmon Salad*
(Cold)

Leftover grilled (& marinated) salmon, cut in bite-sizes, or 1 sm. can salmon, drained & cut up
1 c. corn, drained
Paul Newman's Italian dressing
Cherry tomatoes, halved

Mix and toss lightly.

Ann Cease

Shrimp Louie

Iceberg lettuce
Frozen bay shrimp (sm. ones)
2 bunches green onions
Cilantro
2 avocados
Low-fat thousand island dressing

Thaw out bay shrimp with cool water in colander. Carefully clean all your vegetables. Chop up lettuce into bite-sizes. Finely-chop up green onions and cilantro. Slice avocados into small squares. Sprinkle salt on the avocados (opens the flavor). Toss together and put on plates. Put liberal portions of shrimp on each plate. Put salads in refrigerator for 30 minutes before serving. This chills the plates, brings the shrimp to a good serving temperature and allows the cilantro and onion flavors to open up. Add liberal amount of dressing over top and serve.

This is a fast dish best served on a hot summer day. I recommend serving it with a baguette and a light white wine like pinot grigio or sauvignon blanc.

Tom Lopez

Simple Summer Salad*

25 watermelon balls
25 green grapes
25 cantaloupe balls

Add to 1 can Wilderness peach pie filling. Chill and serve.

Nancy Thiel

Snicker Bar Salad*

6 Granny Smith apples, cut up
6 to 8 lg. Snicker bars, cut up
1 pkg. vanilla instant pudding
1 ctn. Cool Whip

Make the vanilla pudding as directed on package and let set up. Cut the apples and Snicker bars. Mix the pudding and Cool Whip. Add to the apples and Snicker bars. Use a 12- to 16-cup container to mix in.

Wanda Gubrud

Southwest Pasta Salad

1 (12 oz.) box radiotorri pasta, cooked & cooled
1 (8 oz.) ctn. sour cream
1/2 c. Miracle Whip
1/4 c. milk
1 can chili beans in sauce
1/2 pkg. taco seasoning mix
1 (4 oz.) pkg. shredded sharp Cheddar cheese
Diced onion, green pepper, sliced olives (opt.)

Mix together all ingredients, except pasta and cheese; refrigerate. One-half hour before serving, stir sauce mixture into pasta. Toss in shredded cheese.

Debbie Tuck

Sparkling Fruit Salad*

1 c. white grape juice
1 c. 7-Up

Mix in a large bowl (2-quart or larger).

FRUIT BOWL:
 Any combination of your favorite fruit, cut up: strawberries, bananas, apples, oranges, green grapes, red grapes.
 Pour white grape juice and 7-Up over cut-up fruit. Toss to coat all fruit. This helps keep fruit fresh and it does not turn brown or off-color.
 Can be covered and refrigerated, or served immediately.

Judy Gumke

Sunny Summer Tomato Salad*

1/2 c. oil
1/4 c. balsamic vinegar
Fresh basil, to taste
Tomatoes, cubed
Fresh Mozzarella cheese, shredded
Cooked shrimp, cooled
Celery, cut fine

Sunshine Salad*

1 (20 oz.) can pineapple tidbits
1 (11 oz.) can mandarin oranges
1 (3.4 oz.) pkg. instant lemon pudding
1 c. quartered strawberries (or raspberries)
1 c. sliced bananas

Drain pineapple and oranges; reserve liquid. Prepare pudding, using liquid from the fruit instead of milk. Combine pineapple, oranges and strawberries. Gently fold in pudding. Chill at least 2 hours. Add bananas just before serving. Yield: 8 to 10 servings.
 Colorful, nutritional, delicious. Quick and easy!

Phyllis Otterness

Super Strawberry Lettuce

1 head lettuce, chopped or torn
1 sm. red onion, sliced thin
1 qt. fresh strawberries, wash & quarter
1 can mandarin oranges, drained (opt.)

DRESSING:
2 T. raspberry vinegar (or white vinegar)
2 T. poppy seeds
2/3 c. mayonnaise
1/3 c. sugar

Mix dressing in a covered jar. This can be done ahead of serving time. Pour over salad just before serving.

Paula Wright

Swiss Vegetable Medley

1 (16 oz.) bag frozen broccoli, carrots & cauliflower, thawed & drained
1 can cream of mushroom soup
1/3 c. sour cream
1 c. (4 oz.) shredded Swiss cheese
1/4 tsp. black pepper
1 (4 oz.) jar chopped pimento (opt.)
1 can French-fried onions

Combine vegetables, soup, 1/2 cup cheese, sour cream, pimento and 1/2 can French-fried onions. Pour into 1-quart casserole. Bake, covered, at 350° for 30 minutes. Top with remaining cheese and onions. Bake, uncovered, 15 minutes more.
A colorful and very tasty vegetable dish.

Betty Dailey

Tropical Chicken Salad

1 c. cubed, cooked chicken
1 c. chopped celery
1 c. mayonnaise
1/2 tsp. curry powder
1 (20 oz.) can chunk pineapple, drained
2 lg. firm bananas
1 (11 oz.) can mandarin oranges, drained
1/2 c. flaked coconut
Salad greens (opt.)
3/4 c. salted cashews

Place chicken and celery in a large bowl. Combine mayonnaise and curry powder; add to chicken mixture. Mix well. Cover and chill for at least 30 minutes. Before serving, add the pineapple, bananas and coconut. Toss gently. Serve on salad greens. Sprinkle with nuts. Yield: 4 to 6 servings.

From: Taste of Home

Vinaigrette Dressing

3 parts vinegar (balsamic, lemon or lime juice)
1 part oil (olive, canola, sunflower)
Spices & herbs, of choice

Shake and top salad of choice. Leafy greens with tomatoes, celery, carrot slivers, almonds.

From: Radio Show

Zucchini with Zip*

3 to 4 slices bacon
Minced onion, to taste
2 c. sliced (1/4") zucchini
1/2 c. salsa per person

Use frying pan to sauté onion with bacon. Fry until bacon is crisp and onions tender. Drain off grease. Crumble bacon. Add to sliced zucchini; stir together. Add salsa; stir-fry zucchini with bacon, onion and salsa just until zucchini is tender. Serve hot.

A quick and tasty meal with green salad, biscuits or corn bread.

Helen Leach Fitzpatrick

The stomach teaches the hunter to shoot.
Swedish proverb

Notes & Recipes

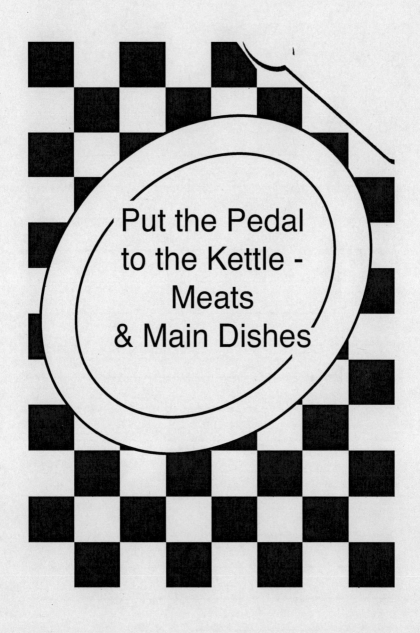

Put the Pedal to the Kettle - Meats & Main Dishes

Notes & Recipes

Put the Pedal to the Kettle – Meats & Main Dishes

Aggie's Enchilada Casserole

Roasted chicken (the kind you buy roasted at the supermarket are fine)
2 cans cream of chicken soup
2 sm. cans chopped mild green chilies (Ortega brand if possible)
2 c. grated sharp Cheddar
1/2 finely-chopped med.-size white onion
2 garlic cloves, minced
1 doz. corn tortillas
1 can mild or med. enchilada sauce (I recommend La Victoria mild traditional enchilada sauce, Chino, CA www.lavicotia.com 800-725-7212)

Empty 2 cans cream of chicken osup, 2 small cans mild green chilies, 1 cup sharp Cheddar cheese, 1 chopped white onion and 2 minced garlic cloves into a large bowl and stir it up good. Shred all of the roasted chicken off the bone and stir it into the bowl of chicken goop. Coat casserole dish with Pam or oil. Cut corn tortillas into long strips, split into two equal portions. Take half the tortilla strips and cover the bottom of the casserole dish with them. Spoon in half the bowl of chicken goop. Spread 1/2 cup sharp Cheddar cheese over the top of the chicken goop. Cover the casserole dish full of goop with the remainder of the tortilla strips, pour the rest of the goop over them and sprinkle the remainder of the cheese on top. Cover casserole dish with plastic shrink-wrap and place in refrigerator for at least 5 hours prior to cooking (this is essential to blend the flavors together). Cook for about 45 minutes at 300°.

Heat 1 can enchilada sauce, ladle over the top of each serving like gravy.

Serve with refried or (use fat-free with a minced garlic clove and some chili powder), black beans and Mexican beer (I prefer Tacate but Corona will do – be sure and serve with a lime). Serve with an avocado slice on top.

Could be a good time to pull out your North Dakota Guacamole.

Tom Lopez

Bacon-Wrapped Chicken

6 boneless, skinless chicken breast halves
1 (8 oz.) ctn. whipped cream cheese with onion & chives
1 T. butter, cubed
Salt, to taste
6 bacon strips

Flatten chicken to 1/2-inch thickness. Spread 3 tablespoons cream cheese over each. Dot with butter and sprinkle with salt; roll up. Wrap each with a bacon strip. Place, seam-side down, in a greased 9x13x2-inch pan. Bake, uncovered, at 400° for 35 to 40 minutes, or until juice runs clear. Broil 6 inches from heat for 5 minutes, or until bacon is crisp.

Sandra Christl

Baked Halibut*

2 lb. halibut (fillets)

Marinate them in 1 cup of sauterne wine (or any other sweet white wine) with one teaspoon of salt for 2 hours or more. Pat dry. Cover both sides with bread crumbs and lay in baking pan.
Mix:
1 c. mayonnaise
1/2 c. sour cream
1/4 c. chopped onion

Spread this mixture on top of fillets. Top with a sprinkle of paprika. Bake in oven at 500° for 15 minutes.

Anita Corby

Baked Potato Soup*

1/3 to 2/3 c. butter
1/3 to 2/3 c. flour
7 c. milk
4 lg. baked potatoes, peeled, cubed
1 c. sour cream
4 green onions, chopped
12 strips bacon or 1 c. chopped ham
1 1/4 c. shredded Cheddar cheese
3/4 tsp. seasoned salt
1/2 tsp. pepper

Melt butter in large kettle, stir in flour, heat until smooth. Gradually add milk, stir until thickened. Add potatoes, onions, bacon or ham. Bring to a boil, stirring constantly. Reduce to simmer. Add cheese and sour cream. Serve. Yield: 8 servings.
Preparation time: 30 minutes.

Judith Krueger

Bar-B-Q Chicken*

1 whole chicken or chicken parts of your choice
1 (16 to 18 oz.) btl. Bar-B-Q sauce
1 sm. yellow chili pepper, diced
1 green pepper, diced
1 c. mushrooms

Place in pot and cook in oven about 2 hours at 350°. Serve over rice. This is so easy and good!

Liane Denton

BBQ Beef and Pork

2 c. chopped onion
1/2 c. brown sugar
3 tsp. chili powder
2 tsp. salt
1 1/2 lb. pork roast, cut up
1 1/2 lb. stew meat
1 tsp. dry mustard
1/4 c. vinegar
2 tsp. Worcestershire sauce
6 oz. tomato paste

Combine all ingredients and place in a Dutch oven. Bake at 325° for 4 hours, stirring occasionally.

Andrea Richman

Bar-B-Q Oven Meat Balls*

2 lb. hamburger
3/4 c. oatmeal
1 1/2 tsp. salt
1/2 tsp. garlic salt
3/4 tsp. pepper
3 T. onion flakes
1 c. half & half

SAUCE:
1 c. ketchup
1 1/2 tsp. vinegar
2 T. sugar
1/2 c. water

Shape meat mixture into meat balls. Put in baking dish. Pour sauce over. Bake at 350° for 1 1/4 hours.
I add more fresh onion besides the onion flakes.

Gladys Ratzlaff

Barbecued Spare Ribs

4 lb. spareribs, cut into serving pieces
1 med. onion, quartered
2 tsp. salt
1/4 tsp. pepper

SAUCE:
1/2 c. cider vinegar
1/2 c. brown sugar
1/2 c. ketchup
1/4 c. chili sauce
1/4 c. Worcestershire sauce
2 T. chopped onion
1 T. lemon juice
1/2 tsp. ground mustard
Dash of cayenne pepper

Place ribs, onion, salt and pepper in a Dutch oven. Add enough water to cover; bring to a boil. Reduce heat and simmer until tender.
Sauce: Combine ingredients in a saucepan; simmer until slightly thickened.
Drain ribs. Place on broiler pan, brush with sauce. Broil 5 minutes on each side, brush with sauce frequently. Yield: 4 servings.
Refrigerate unused sauce, may be used on other meats or a dipping sauce.
Lois Berndt

Beef Stroganoff Sandwich*

2 lb. ground beef
1/2 c. chopped onion
1 tsp. salt
1/2 tsp. garlic powder
1/2 tsp. pepper
1 loaf French bread
Butter or margarine
2 c. (16 oz.) sour cream
2 tomatoes, seeded & diced
1 green pepper, diced
2 c. shredded Cheddar cheese

Brown beef and onions. Add salt, garlic powder and pepper. Cut bread in half, butter bread and place on baking sheet. Stir sour cream into meat mixture. Spoon on bread. Sprinkle with tomato and green pepper. Top with cheese. Bake at 350° for 20 minutes.
Esther Haa

Beef Taco Bake*

1 lb. ground beef, cooked
1 can condensed tomato soup
1 c. salsa or picante sauce
1 c. shredded Cheddar cheese
1/2 c. milk
6 to 8 flour tortillas, cut into 1" pieces (use 6" or 8" size), you can use corn tortillas if you like

Cook beef until browned. Drain off any fat. Add soup, salsa and milk. Add cut up tortillas and 1/2 cup cheese. Mix and place in shallow 2-quart baking dish. Cover and bake at 400° for 30 minutes, or until hot. Sprinkle with remaining cheese and return to oven until cheese is melted.
Marlis Headland

Belgian Pork with Sauerkraut*

1 lb. lean center cut pork chops, cut 1/4" to 1/2"
Salt, to taste
Pepper, to taste
2 c. sauerkraut, undrained
1 med. onion, sliced thin
1 lg. apple, sliced thin
2 T. parsley, chopped
2 tsp. brown sugar
1/2 tsp. allspice
1/2 tsp. salt

Spray a large skillet with nonstick vegetable cooking spray. Brown chops on both sides over medium heat; sprinkle with salt and pepper to taste. Preheat oven to 350°. In an 8-inch square baking dish, toss sauerkraut, onion, 1/2 the apple slices, parsley, brown sugar, allspice and 1/2 teaspoon salt. Lay pork chops on top of sauerkraut. Top with remaining apple slices. Cover and bake at 350° for 1 hour, or until pork is tender. Yield: 4 servings.
Serve with boiled new potatoes and green beans.

Sandy DalBello

Best-Ever Meat Loaf*

1 (11 1/8 oz.) can Campbell's condensed Italian tomato soup
2 lb. ground beef
1 pouch Campbell's dry onion soup & recipe mix
1/2 c. dry bread crumbs
1 egg, beaten
1/4 c. water

Mix 1/2 cup Italian tomato soup, beef, soup mix, bread crumbs and egg thoroughly. In baking pan, shape firmly into 4x8-inch loaf. Bake at 350° for 1 1/4 hours, or until meat loaf is done (160°). In saucepan, mix 2 tablespoons drippings, remaining soup and water. Heat through. Serve with meat loaf. If desired, garnish with baby corn, zucchini, tomatoes and fresh sage. Yield: 8 servings.
Preparation time: 10 minutes. Cook time: 1 hour and 20 minutes.

From: Campbell's Back Label Cookbook

The Lord gives every bird its food, but He does not cast it into the nest.
Swedish proverb

Black Bean Soup*

2 (15 oz.) cans black beans
1 1/2 c. vegetable or chicken broth
1 c. thick & chunky salsa
1 tsp. ground cumin
1/2 tsp. red pepper
1/2 tsp. chopped garlic
1/3 c. diced onion

In an electric food processor or blender, combine beans and cumin. Blend until fairly smooth. Heat bean mixture in medium saucepan over medium heat, along with spices, salsa and onion until thoroughly heated.
May be served with a dollop of plain yogurt or sour cream or with a sprinkling of grated sharp Cheddar cheese and a few crushed tortilla chips.

Claudia Richman Nelson

Brett's Chicken and Herb Casserole*

1/2 lb. hamburger, browned
3/4 pkg. noodles, cooked as directed
1 can chicken & herb soup
1/3 can water
1/2 c. Parmesan cheese, for topping

Mix together. Heat in microwave until hot. Top with Parmesan cheese. Ready to go!

Brett Cease

Broccoli-Cheese Casserole*

1 (8 oz.) pkg. Uncle Ben's instant wild rice
1 (16 oz.) pkg. frozen, chopped broccoli
1 (8 oz.) jar Cheez Whiz
1 can cream of mushroom soup

Cook rice according to package. Add broccoli, Cheez Whiz and soup. Cook at 400° for 30 minutes.

Val Moritz

Plain cooking cannot be entrusted to plain cooks.
Countess Morphy

Bubble Pizza*

2 tubes refrigerated buttermilk biscuits
1 (15 oz.) can pizza sauce
1 lb. hamburger, crumbled, browned & drained
1 1/2 c. (6 oz.) shredded Mozzarella cheese
1 c. (4 oz.) shredded Cheddar cheese

Stir the pizza sauce into the browned hamburger. Quarter the biscuits; put into greased 9x13-inch baking pan. Top with meat mixture. Bake, uncovered, at 400° for 20 minutes, or until biscuits look done, then quickly sprinkle with the cheese and bake a little more so it melts. Let stand 5 to 10 minutes before serving.

You can add green pepper, onions, black olives, mushrooms, etc., if you wish.

Cake Pan Potatoes

4 lg. potatoes
1 tsp. salt
1/8 tsp. pepper
3/4 c. shredded sharp cheese (I use Cheddar)
3 T. butter or margarine
1/4 c. finely-chopped onion
1/3 c. light cream
Parsley, for garnish

Peel potatoes and cut into finger like strips, about 1/4-inch wide. Put potatoes in an 8 1/2 x 1 1/4-inch round baking dish. Sprinkle with salt, pepper and cheese. Dot with butter and onion. Pour cream over the top. Cover dish tightly with foil. Bake in a hot oven at 425° for 50 minutes, or until tender. Yield: about 6 cups.

Enjoy!

Paulette Dew

Never put all your eggs in one basket.
Proverb

Carol's One-Step Lasagna*

1 lb. hamburger
1 onion
1 tsp. salt

Brown hamburger with onion and salt; set aside.

1 (15 oz.) jar spaghetti sauce
1 (8 oz.) can tomato sauce
1 T. dried parsley
6 to 8 lasagna noodles, uncooked
16 oz. cottage cheese
2 eggs
1/4 c. Parmesan cheese
8 oz. Mozzarella cheese
1 c. water
1/4 c. grated Parmesan cheese

Mix cottage cheese, egg and the first 1/4 cup Parmesan cheese; set aside. Spread 1/2 cup sauce on the bottom of greased 9x13-inch pan. Layer noodles, hamburger, cottage cheese, Mozzarella cheese, and sauce. Repeat. Keep noodles 1/2 inch from the sides. Pour 1 cup of water over all and then remaining Parmesan cheese over it. Cover with foil. Bake at 350° for 1 hour. Remove foil and bake 15 minutes more. Cool 15 minutes before serving. Yield: 8 to 12 servings.

Carol Grindberg

Cheeseburger Bake*

1 1/2 lb. ground beef
1 1/2 tsp. onion powder
1/2 tsp. garlic powder
1/2 tsp. black pepper
1/3 c. ketchup
1 1/2 c. shredded Cheddar
1 (7 1/2 oz.) pkg. (10 biscuits) refrigerated biscuits

Brown ground beef with spices. Drain fat. Add ketchup and cheese. Mix thoroughly and pour in 8-inch sprayed baking dish. Place biscuits on top (flatten if necessary). Bake for 8 to 10 minutes at 350° until biscuits are golden brown.

Joan Halland

Some books are to be tasted, others to be swallowed, and some are to be chewed and digested.
Francis Bacon

Cheeseburger Soup

1/2 lb. ground beef
3/4 c. chopped onion
3/4 c. celery, chopped
3/4 c. carrots, cut up
1 tsp. basil
1 tsp. parsley
4 T. butter, divided by 1/3's
3 c. chicken broth
4 c. diced, raw potatoes
1/4 c. flour
2 c. shredded Cheddar cheese
1 1/2 c. milk
3/4 tsp. salt
1/2 tsp. pepper
1/4 c. sour cream

Sauté meat; drain and set aside. Add 1 tablespoon butter to vegetables and sauté until done, about 10 minutes. Add broth and potatoes; bring to boil. Simmer until potatoes are done. Melt rest of the butter in a skillet and add flour. Cook until smooth and creamy. Add milk and stir for 3 to 5 minutes, until bubbly. Then add this to rest of the ingredients. Bring to a boil. Cook 2 minutes, reduce heat. Add cheese, salt and pepper. Cook until cheese melts. Serve in preheated bowls. Garnish soup with sour cream as it is served.

Liane Denton

Cheesy Vegetable Soup*

2 cans chicken broth
2 cans water
1 chopped onion
1 c. chopped potatoes
1 c. chopped carrots

Let cook for 10 to 15 minutes. Add one 16-ounce bag of California Blend frozen vegetables. Cook until tender. Add 2 cans cream of chicken soup. Add 1 pound Velveeta cheese, cut in chunks. Mix and simmer 10 minutes
Optional: Add 1 cup celery with the potatoes and carrots.

Arla Kapaun

My books are water; those of great geniuses are wine. Everybody drinks water.
Mark Twain

Chicken Casserole
(Tower City Version)

2 pkg. Stove Top dressing
2 chicken bouillon cubes
2 c. hot water
4 to 5 chicken breasts, cooked
   & cut in small pieces
1 can cream of chicken soup
1 can cream of celery soup
1 sm. ctn. sour cream
1 c. milk
1/2 c. margarine

Mix dressing mixes with packets of spices in large bowl. Add bouillon cubes in hot water. Stir until moist and spread in 9x13-inch pan. Mix soups, sour cream, 1 cup milk and margarine well. Place chicken pieces on dressing mixture. Pour liquid soup mixture over chicken and dressing. Bake at 350° for 1 hour, or more.

Large casserole, should serve 8 or more. Should be lightly browned on top.

Jeanne Kapaun

Chicken Casserole
(Valley City Version)

5 c. cut-up cooked chicken
   breasts
2 cans cream of chicken soup
1 (13 oz.) can Carnation
   evaporated milk
1 can sliced water chestnuts

Mix above together.

2 pkg. Stove Top cornbread
   stuffing (or herbed)
1 c. melted margarine

Mix together.
Put 1/2 of crumbs in bottom of 9x13-inch pan. Pat down and refrigerate 1 hour. Put chicken mix on top. Put other 1/2 crumbs on top of chicken. Bake, covered, at 325° for 35 to 45 minutes.

Can be frozen before baking, thaw a day in refrigerator before baking. Serve with cranberries.

Mary Tangen

Chicken Cutlets with Couscous and Toasted Pine Nuts

CHICKEN:
Boneless chicken breast
Progresso Italian bread crumbs (important as the crumbs have most of the seasoning)

Garlic
1 egg
Extra-virgin olive oil

COUSCOUS:
1 box Near East brand couscous with toasted pine nuts
Chopped green onions
Fat-free chicken broth

Fresh pine nuts
Olive oil as per instructions (the recipe on the box calls for water but it's way better with the fat-free chicken broth)

Wash chicken breasts. Pound the hell out of the breast with a tenderizer mallet until the breast is flat and you're sure the chicken is dead. Break 1 egg in a bowl. Put a liberal amount of bread crumbs on a plate. Heat up a bit of olive oil in a pan at medium heat. Add 3 garlic cloves strained through a garlic press. Take the breast, dip it in the egg, cover it in bread crumbs and cook both sides until golden brown.

Couscous: Read the box, use fat-free chicken broth instead of water. Add green onions and pine nuts. Serve chicken breasts over the couscous.

Tom Lopez

Chicken with Biscuits*

1 (19 oz.) can chunky chicken vegetable soup
1 c. chopped, cooked chicken or 1 (5 oz.) can chunk-style chicken

1 c. shredded Monterey Jack cheese (4 oz.)
Biscuits (refrigerated, in a roll), bake separately, then place on top of hot soup

In a medium saucepan, combine soup, chicken and cheese. Cook over medium heat until cheese melts and mixture is hot, stirring occasionally.

To serve, spoon chicken mixture into 3 individual bowls. Top with biscuits.

Diane Landgrebe

Chicken Enchilada Soup*

1 can cream of chicken soup
1 can Cheddar cheese soup
1 can enchilada sauce
2 2/3 c. milk
6 oz. picante sauce
1 (10 oz.) can chicken

Mix all ingredients in large saucepan. Cook over medium-high heat until heated thoroughly, about 30 minutes. Or put in crock-pot on low for 4 to 5 hours, stirring occasionally. Serve with grated cheese and tortilla chips.

Andrea Richman

Chicken Huntington*

3 c. cooked chicken
2 c. macaroni (ND product)
1 c. chicken broth
1 can cream of mushroom soup
4 T. butter
4 T. flour
1 c. celery, cut fine
2 c. Velveeta cheese, cut in small cubes
Pimento, to taste (opt.)
Salt & pepper, to taste
Crushed potato chips

Melt butter. Add flour mix. Add broth and soup. Bring to a simmer. Place chicken, macaroni, celery and cheese in a 9x13-inch pan. Cover with sauce, if dry, add more broth. Cover with potato chips. Bake at 325° for 1 hour. This recipe is served each year at our fall bazaar.

Lois Berndt

Chicken Parmesan*

4 to 6 chicken breasts, uncooked
1 (28 oz.) jar spaghetti sauce
2 T. Parmesan cheese
1 to 2 c. shredded Mozzarella cheese
8 to 10 oz. spaghetti, prepared as directed on pkg.

Lay chicken breasts in 8x10-inch casserole dish. Cover with prepared spaghetti sauce. Sprinkle with Parmesan cheese. Bake for 30 to 45 minutes, until bubbly and test cheese for doneness. Sprinkle with Mozzarella cheese. Heat for 5 to 10 minutes longer until cheese is melted. Serve over cooked spaghetti!

My family loves this quick and easy dish. Have shared it with my FACS students and many brides!!

Margaret Vollmuth

Chicken Salad Tacos*

1/3 c. mayonnaise
1/3 c. sour cream
2 T. chopped fresh cilantro
1 T. lime juice
2 tsp. taco seasoning
1 whole cooked chicken breast, chopped
6 taco shells

In a small bowl, combine mayonnaise, sour cream, cilantro, lime juice and taco seasoning. Stir in chicken. Chill up to 24 hours. Serve on warm tortilla shells. Yield: 2 to 4 servings.

Top these tasty tacos with chopped tomato, onions, olives or shredded cheese.

From: American Profile

Chicken Quesadillas*

2 chicken breasts, cooked & shredded
1 1/3 c. chunky salsa
1 1/3 c. shredded Monterey Jack cheese
1/2 c. finely-chopped green onion
12 flour tortilla shells

Combine chicken, salsa, cheese and onion. Spread mixture on tortilla shell. Cover with another shell. Spray skillet with nonstick cooking spray. Place one tortilla stack in a large skillet over medium heat. Cover and cook 2 minutes. Turn and cook 1 to 2 minutes longer, or until cheese is melted. Serve with sour cream, lettuce, salsa, etc. Yield: 6 small quesadillas.

Mary Richman

Chicken Tortilla Soup*

2 c. water
3 T. chicken bouillon
2 chicken breasts, diced
1 can Cheddar cheese soup
1 can cream of chicken soup
1 (8 oz.) jar mild salsa
1 (8 oz.) pkg. shredded cheese

Add bouillon to water, add chicken breasts. Cook until meat is done. Add soups, salsa and cheese. Simmer on low heat until cheese melts. Serve with tortilla chips.

Very good and easy, too!

Carmen Gubrud

Chicken Tortilla Soup*

1 can mild enchilada soup
1 can cream of chicken soup
1 can nacho fiesta cheese soup
2 c. milk
2 c. shredded Cheddar cheese
1 can chicken

Open all cans of soup and pour into a 2-quart saucepan. Stir in the milk; mix. Add chicken and cheese. Heat over medium heat until hot. Try not to let it boil. Can use hot enchilada sauce if you like. Yield: 6 servings.

Nancy King

Cincinnati Chili Soup

2 T. salad oil
2 c. diced onion
4 tsp. minced onion
1 1/2 lb. ground beef
1 (14 to 16 oz.) can diced tomatoes
2 tsp. salt
1 to 2 tsp. chili powder
1/2 to 1 tsp. ground red pepper
1/4 tsp. cumin
1/8 tsp. allspice
Pinch of cloves
3 c. tomato juice
1 (14 oz.) can beef broth
1 (28 oz.) can kidney beans, drained
1 c. spaghetti, broken
1 T. cider vinegar
1 c. shredded Cheddar cheese
1/2 c. finely-chopped onion

In a large stockpot, heat oil over high heat. Add onions and garlic; cook, stirring until onions are translucent, about 3 minutes. Add beef, stirring until browned, about 10 minutes. Drain off excess liquid. Add tomatoes and seasonings. Stir, add tomato juice, beef broth and kidney beans. Bring to boil; reduce heat and simmer 45 minutes. Bring to boil again and add spaghetti, broken in 1-inch pieces. Reduce heat and simmer until spaghetti is cooked, 15 to 20 minutes. Stir in vinegar, cook 1 minute more.
Serve in bowl with a sprinkle of shredded cheese and onion. Yield: 12 cups.

Lila Hutchinson

Cola Chicken*

4 chicken breasts, placed in casserole

Mix together:
1 can cream of mushroom soup
1/2 can diet Cola
2 T. dried onion flakes
1 T. parsley

Pour over chicken. Cover, bake at 350° for 35 to 45 minutes. Makes a great gravy to pour over rice or potatoes.

Tammy Buhr Erickson

Cottage Cheese Pocket Recipe

1 c. flour
1 tsp. salt
2 eggs
1 1/2 c. cottage cheese (dry-curd)
1 sm. onion, finely chopped
1 piece of parsley, finely cut (opt.)
Salt & pepper, to taste
1 egg

Mix and add cold water or milk to make a stiff dough. Roll dough on floured board as thin as pie crust and cut into 3-inch squares.

Mix and put about 1 tablespoon of this cheese on each square of dough. Fold square in half and squeeze shut with the fingers. Now take 8 cups water, a piece of parsley, salt to taste and put into a kettle and boil. Add the pockets to the water and boil slowly for 15 minutes. Fry an onion or dry, cubed bread in 2 tablespoons lard in a pan. Add fried onions and bread crumbs to drained pockets when they are done. Fry leftover pockets for another meal.

Leona Schumacher Schock

Crab Alfredo*

1 pt. half & half
1 stick butter
2 to 3 T. cream cheese
1/2 to 3/4 c. Parmesan cheese
1 tsp. garlic powder
1 pkg. imitation crab or thawed unbreaded shrimp

Melt butter; add cream cheese until smooth. Add half & half and simmer gently. Add crab and shrimp. Heat thoroughly. Add Parmesan cheese now or as a garnish. Serve over angel hair pasta.

Joan Halland

Creamed Chicken*

1 lb. boneless, skinless chicken breasts, cut into 1/2" strips
1 T. vegetable oil
1 (10 3/4 oz.) can condensed cream of chicken soup, undiluted
1 c. water
1/4 tsp. salt
Pepper, to taste
1/2 c. sour cream
English muffins, split & toasted
Cayenne pepper or paprika

In a large skillet, sauté the chicken in oil until no longer pink. Stir in the soup, water, salt and pepper. Bring to a boil. Remove from the heat and stir in sour cream. Serve over toasted English muffins. Sprinkle with cayenne or paprika. Yield: 4 servings.

For faster preparation time: Use cooked chicken, skip the oil, proceed as listed above.

Debra Baker

Easy Chicken A La King*

1 (10 3/4 oz.) can cream of chicken soup, undiluted
1/4 c. milk
1 c. chopped, cooked chicken (may substitute canned chicken or frozen, cooked chicken strips)
1/4 c. frozen peas
1 (2 oz.) jar diced pimento, drained
1 (4 oz.) can whole mushrooms, drained
1/2 tsp. salt
1/2 tsp. pepper
Chow mein noodles, hot cooked rice or toast

Combine soup, milk, chicken, peas, pimento and mushrooms in a heavy saucepan; cook over low heat for 6 to 8 minutes. Season with salt and pepper. Cook for additional 2 to 4 minutes, stir often during cooking process. Serve over noodles, rice or toast.

Lyn Nicols,
The Forum

Make It Easy Chicken

1 Reynolds Oven Bag, large size (14"x20")
2 T. flour
1 env. golden onion soup mix
1 c. water
3 med. carrots, cut in chunks
2 med. red potatoes, cut in wedges
1 med. green bell pepper, cubed
6 chicken pieces, skin removed
Seasoned salt & pepper

Preheat oven to 350°. Shake flour in Reynolds Oven Bag; place in 9x13x2-inch baking pan. Add onion soup mix and water to oven bag. Squeeze oven bag to blend in flour. Add carrots, potatoes and green pepper to oven pan. Turn oven bag to coat ingredients with sauce. Sprinkle chicken with seasonings; add to oven bag. Arrange chicken and vegetable in an even layer in oven bag. Close oven bag with nylon tie; cut six 1/2-inch slits on top. Bake for 55 to 60 minutes, or until chicken is tender. Yield: 4 servings.

From Reynolds Oven Bags Label

Bread and books: food for the body and food the soul –
what could be more worthy of our respect, and even love?
Salman Rushdie

Chili Verde

4 T. cooking oil
4 lb. boneless pork, cubed
1/4 c. flour
1 (4 oz.) can chopped green chilies
1/2 tsp. ground cumin
1/4 tsp. salt
1/4 tsp. pepper
3 minced garlic cloves
1/2 c. parsley
1/2 to 1 c. prepared salsa
1 (14 1/2 oz.) can chicken broth
Flour tortillas, warmed

In Dutch oven, heat oil over medium-high. Add cubed pork and stir until lightly browned. Sprinkle flour over meat; mix well. Add chilies, cumin, salt, pepper, garlic, parsley, salsa and broth. Cover and simmer 1 1/2 hours. Serve with warm tortillas.

If you like hot chili, use a medium or hot salsa.

Doris Sauerland

Crock-Pot Beef Stew

3 carrots, sliced
3 potatoes, cubed
2 lb. beef cubes
1 c. water or beef stock
1 tsp. Worcestershire sauce
1 clove garlic
1 bay leaf
Salt & pepper
3 sm. onions, sliced
1 stalk celery & tops

Mix all. Cover crock-pot and set on low for 10 to 12 hours, or high 5 to 6 hours.

Vi Egan

Cruise Control Pork Tenderloin

This is about as fancy as you dare get in the down-home Midwest, but it's OK if the pork tenderloin is from a native Iowa hog. The long cooking time will let you put a lot of prairie miles behind you. Just set the cruise control, line up your hood ornament with a distant landmark like the Nebraska State Capitol, and set a timer to wake you up when dinner is ready.

Distance: 250 miles.

3 T. Dijon mustard
2 T. dry white wine
1/2 c. minced red onion
2 tsp. dried rosemary, crushed
Salt & pepper, to taste
1 (1 1/2 to 2 lb.) pork tenderloin, butterflied

At home or on the road, blend mustard, wine, onion and seasonings. Spread split surface of tenderloin with the mixture and press lightly together, then wrap with foil. Find a medium-hot spot on the engine and turn once during cooking. Total cooking time should be about 4 1/2 hours.

From The One and Only Guide to Cooking on your Car Engine. Manifold Destiny.

By: Chris Maynard,
Bill Scheller

Easy Hot Dish*

1 lb. hamburger
1 sm. onion
1 can pork & beans
1 pt. stewed tomatoes
2 T. brown sugar
1/3 lb. bacon, cut up & uncooked
1/4 c. ketchup
1 c. macaroni, uncooked
Salt & pepper, to taste

Brown hamburger and chopped onion; drain off grease. Add all ingredients to a covered casserole or small covered roaster pan. Mix well. Bake for 1 hour at 375°. Yield: 6 to 8 servings.

Yes – the bacon and macaroni go in to the mix raw. I use Bush's original baked beans. Be sure to use juice and all on the stewed tomatoes. This recipe doubles very well. I melt slices of Velveeta or American cheese on top before using or sprinkle with Parmesan cheese. If you like green or red peppers, chop and add tablespoon to the mix before cooking.

Dean Sauer

Fake Lasagna*

1/2 pkg. egg noodles
1 c. milk
2 eggs
1 tsp. salt
1 lb. hamburger
Chopped onion, to taste
1 (16 oz.) jar tomato sauce
1/2 tsp. garlic salt
1/2 tsp. Italian seasoning
1/2 tsp. oregano
1/4 tsp. pepper
Shredded Cheddar & Mozzarella cheese

Cook egg noodles according to package directions. Cool and put in greased 9x13-inch pan. Beat milk, eggs and salt; pour over noodles. Brown hamburger and onions. Mix tomato sauce, garlic salt, Italian seasoning, oregano and pepper in saucepan; simmer 10 minutes. Pour hamburger and onions and sauce over noodles. Cover with shredded cheese. Bake at 350° for 20 to 25 minutes.

Arlene Cease,
Contributed by B. Cudmore in A Taste of Faith Cookbook,
Bagley, MN

Foolproof Swiss Steak*

1 Reynolds Oven Bag, large size (14"x20")
2 T. flour
2 (14 1/2 oz.) cans Italian stewed tomatoes
2 tsp. sugar
1 tsp. prepared mustard
1/2 tsp. salt
1/4 tsp. pepper
1 to 1 1/2 lb. boneless beef round steak (1/2" thick)

Preheat oven to 350°. Shake flour in Reynolds Oven Bag; place in 9x13x2-inch baking pan. Add tomatoes, sugar, mustard, salt and pepper to oven bag. Squeeze oven bag to blend in flour. Pound steak in 1/8- to 1/4-inch thickness, using a meat mallet or rolling pin. Cut steak in 4 pieces. Add steak to oven bag. Turn oven bag to coat steak with sauce. Arrange steak in an even layer in oven bag. Close oven bag with nylon tie. Cut six 1/2-inch slits on top. Bake for 45 to 50 minutes, or until steak is tender. Yield: 4 servings.

From Reynolds Oven Bag Label

Forgotten Chicken

1 1/2 c. raw rice (white or a blend)
Chicken breasts, enough to cover pan
1 can mushroom soup, mixed with 1 1/2 c. milk
1 env. dry onion soup mix

Grease 9x13-inch pan and spread raw rice over bottom. Lay raw chicken breast over and pour mixture over the top. Cover tightly with foil. Bake for 2 to 2 1/2 hours at 350°.

Option: I also like to wrap dried beef around the chicken breast.

Diane Kohler

Four-Minute Dumplings*
(Small Recipe)

1 egg
Scant 1/2 c. water, just enough to make batter soft enough to drop from spoon
1 c. flour
2 tsp. baking powder
1/2 tsp. salt

Sift flour with baking powder and salt into bowl. Add beaten egg and water. Stir. Drop into boiling soup. Cover and boil 4 minutes. Serve at once.

Laura Stowman

Garlicky Chicken Breasts*

6 boneless, skinless chicken breasts (about 2 lb.)
1/2 c. grated Parmesan cheese
1 env. Good Seasons roasted garlic or Italian salad dressing mix

Mix together dressing mix and Parmesan cheese. Moisten chicken breasts in water; dip in dressing mixture. Place in shallow baking dish. Bake at 400° for about 20 to 30 minutes (depending on size of chicken breasts).

Penny Zaun

Garrison Keillor's Family Meat Loaf

1 1/2 lb. lean ground beef
3 slices bread, diced
1/2 c. milk
2 eggs, beaten
1/4 c. minced onion
1/4 tsp. pepper
1/4 tsp. celery salt
1/4 tsp. garlic salt
1/4 tsp. dried mustard
1/4 tsp. sage

Bake in a loaf pan for 1 1/2 hours at 350°. You can put ketchup on the top if you wish.

The Betty Crocker recipe calls for one pound of ground beef, 1/4 pound lean ground pork and 1/4 pound ground veal.

And Worcestershire sauce, which usually my mother skips. Maybe nowadays she uses it, though. In recent years, her children have accompanied her on trips to luxurious places – the Ritz Hotel in London, the Sherry Netherland in New York—and perhaps Worcestershire is now on her list.

All I cared about was that she had made tea cookies for me and read to me from her favorite book.
It was enough to prove that she liked me.
Maya Angelou

General Tso's Chicken
(A Chinese-Style Favorite)

4 lg. chicken breasts
2 stalks celery, cut in chunks
1 red or green pepper, cut in chunks
1 sm. onion, cut in chunks
1/2 c. cut carrots

SAUCE:
3 T. soy sauce
3/4 c. ketchup
1 c. honey
2 T. vegetable oil
2 tsp. minced onion

Place chicken breasts and vegetables in a single layer in a 9x13-inch pan or open roaster. Combine sauce ingredients and pour over the ingredients in the roaster. Bake, uncovered, 1 to 1 1/2 hours at 325°. While the main dish bakes, prepare the rice for a complete meal. Yield: 4 servings.

Chicken breasts may be cut into bite-size pieces and cooking time shortened by half. I like to cut them up after cooking to retain juiciness and place back into the sauce for serving.

Coni Horsager

Grandma's Delicious Swiss Steak with Dumplings

2 lb. round steak, 3/4" thick
1/3 c. flour

Cut round steak into serving pieces. Roll in flour. Brown in skillet, both sides in 2 tablespoons oil. Transfer to greased 2 1/2-quart baking dish.
Mix together:

1 1/2 c. water
1/2 tsp. salt
1/8 tsp. pepper

Heat before pouring over steak in baking dish. Cover and bake for 1 hour at 350°.

DUMPLINGS:
1/2 c. dry bread crumbs
5 T. melted butter or margarine
1 1/3 c. flour
2 tsp. baking powder
1/2 tsp. poultry seasoning
1/2 tsp. salt
2/3 c. milk

Combine in small bowl, 2 tablespoons butter first. Combine rest in bowl with remaining butter. Drop rounded tablespoon into bowl with crumbs, then place dumplings over steak. Remove cover form large baking pan. Bake at 400° for 20 to 30 minutes, until dumplings are lightly browned and check done with a toothpick. Dumplings are done when toothpick comes out clean. Yield: 6 to 8 servings.

Takes time, but delicious results!

Arla Kapaun

Grand Slam Chili*

This is the recipe Beltrami Electric Cooperative entered in the 2002 United Way Chili Cook-off. The recipe comes compliments of Joanne Torfin. The Lit'l Smokies were added by Beltrami Electric to stick with the event's American theme.

2 lb. lean ground beef
1 med. onion, chopped
13 oz. tomato sauce
7 1/2 oz. tomato paste
2 oz. tomato juice
20 oz. kidney beans
1/3 tsp. ground oregano
1/2 tsp. Lawry's seasoning salt
2 c. water
2 T. chili powder
Lit'l Smokies

Brown ground beef and onion. Add remaining ingredients and simmer for 1 hour. Yield: 6 servings.

From: Beltrami Electric Cooperative

Gourmet Tomato Soup*

3/4 c. chopped onion
2/3 c. butter
3/4 tsp. dill seed
1 tsp. dill weed
1 tsp. oregano
1/4 c. flour
3 (14.5 oz.) cans Hunt's diced tomatoes
2 (14 oz.) cans Swanson's chicken broth
1 c. cream
2 T. sugar

Sauté onion in butter. Add seasonings, stir in flour. Add tomatoes and chicken broth. Cook 15 minutes. Add cream and sugar. Serve.
I make this a lot, it is wonderful and fast.

Dorothy Enger

Hamburger Dill Casserole

1 lb. ground beef, browned & seasoned
1 c. celery, diced
1 c. potatoes, diced
1 sm. onion, chopped
1 c. carrots, sliced
1 can tomato bisque soup

Place vegetables in bottom of (sprayed with oil) casserole or 9x9-inch pan. Top with hamburger, then tomato soup. Sprinkle generously with dill weed. Bake for 1 hour at 350°, covered. Top with buttermilk biscuits, uncovered. Bake for 15 minutes longer.

Joyce Johnson

High Hat

1 med.-sized onion, diced
1/2 bell pepper, diced
1 1/2 lb. hamburger (salt & pepper)
1 can tomato soup (no milk)
1 can hot water (out of soup can)
1 can Riviera mushroom steak sauce (little water to rinse can)
3 c. egg noodles
1 sm. can pitted olives
2/3 c. grated cheese (American or Tillamook or sliced strips of Mozzarella)
1 can mushrooms
1 clove garlic, diced
Pinch of Italian seasoning on meat when you brown it

Brown hamburger with Italian seasoning and the green pepper, onion, garlic, salt and pepper. Add soup, water, mushroom sauce, olives and mushrooms to meat mixture. When all browned, pour over <u>dry noodles</u> and stir. Pour in long pan (about 9x13-inch), cheese on top. Bake, covered (foil), at 325° for 45 minutes. Yield: about 6 servings.

I like this because you don't need to cook the noodles first, plus they are always done just right. I've been making this for forty years and it is always well received.

Norma Stephens

Honey-Lemon Chicken*

4 skinless, boneless chicken breast halves
2 T. honey
1/2 tsp. dried rosemary leaves
1/4 tsp. salt
Natural Pam lemon-flavor seasoning spray

Preheat broiler. Spray broiling pan rack with seasoning spray. Place chicken on rack. Spray top of each breast with Pam for one second. Broil 10 minutes. Meanwhile, in a cup, mix remaining ingredients. Remove pan from oven; spray both sides of chicken generously with Pam, about 1 second per side. Turn chicken. Broil 10 minutes longer, basting occasionally with honey mixture during last 5 minutes of cooking time. Yield: 4 servings.

Karen Richman

Italian Meat Loaf Pie*

1 lb. ground beef
1 egg
1/3 c. chopped onion
3/4 c. corn flake crumbs
2 T. ketchup
1 tsp. Italian seasoning
Dash of pepper
Dash of garlic powder

FILLING:
1/2 c. sliced black olives, drained
1 1/2 c. shredded Mozzarella cheese
1 (4 oz.) can sliced mushrooms, drained
1/4 c. corn flake crumbs
1 T. melted margarine

Preheat oven to 400°. Combine meat, egg, onion, corn flake crumbs, ketchup and seasonings. Press into the bottom and sides of a 9-inch pie plate. Bake at 400° for 15 minutes. Remove the meat shell from the oven and reduce the temperature to 350°.

Filling: Combine the olives, cheese and mushrooms. Toss lightly and spoon into the hot meat shell. Melt the margarine and toss with 1/4 cup corn flakes. Sprinkle the crumbs over the cheese mixture and return the pie to the oven for 10 minutes. Yield: 6 servings.

Optional Garnish: Grated Parmesan cheese.
Serving Suggestion: Works well with a cooked pasta and salad.

Coni Horsager

Italian Subs

- 1/3 c. olive oil
- 4 1/2 tsp. vinegar (white/cider)
- 1 T. dried parsley flakes
- 2/3 garlic cloves, minced
- 1 (2 1/4 oz.) can sliced ripe olives
- 1/2 c. chopped stuffed olives
- 6 sub sandwich buns
- Sliced salami
- Provolone cheese
- Sliced ham
- Lettuce leaves

In a bowl, combine oil, vinegar, parsley and garlic. Stir in olives. Cover and refrigerate for a few hours or overnight. Place about 2 tablespoons of this mixture on the bottom of a bun. Layer with meats, cheese and lettuce. Add top of bun and serve. Serve with mustard and mayonnaise.

Our new daughter-in-law made these and they were delicious!!

Margaret Vollmuth

Lentil Soup

- 1 T. vegetable oil
- 1 lg. carrot, scraped & chopped small (about 1/2 c.)
- 1 lg. onion, peeled & chopped small (about 1 c.)
- 1 or 2 garlic cloves, minced
- 1/2 tsp. ground cumin
- 1/2 c. brown lentils, rinsed
- 4 c. water
- 1/2 c. chopped, canned tomatoes
- 1/2 pkg. frozen, chopped spinach
- 2 lg. Knorr chicken bouillon cubes

In heavy saucepan heat the oil to sizzling. Add the carrot, onion and garlic; cook, stirring for about 3 minutes. Add the cumin and stir well into the oil. Stir in the lentils, water and tomatoes. Cover the pan and bring the mixture to a boil over high heat. Immediately reduce the heat to moderately low. Stir the soup and partially cover. Let the soup simmer for 30 to 35 minutes, stirring it occasionally and keeping an eye on the pot to be sure it is simmering, not boiling. If the lentils are fairly soft, stir in the chopped spinach and the bouillon cubes. Cook an additional 10 minutes. Serve.

I tend to double the recipe and freeze it...it holds its flavor well, and can be served over couscous as an entrée.

Amanda Richman

Linguine with Garlic Clam Sauce*

8 oz. linguine
2 to 3 cloves garlic, minced
5 T. butter or margarine
1/4 c. vegetable oil
1 T. flour
2 (6 1/2 oz.) cans minced clams
1 c. shredded Monterey Jack cheese
1/4 c. minced fresh parsley

Cook linguine. In skillet, sauté garlic in butter and oil until golden. Stir in flour until blended. Drain clams, reserving juice; set clams aside. Gradually add juice to skillet. Bring to a boil; cook and stir for 2 minutes, or until thickened. Reduce heat. Stir in clams, cheese, and parsley. Cook until cheese is melted and sauce is thickened. Drain linguine and top with clam sauce. Yield: 4 servings.

Mary Richman

Mexican Lasagna

1 lb. lean ground beef
1 (16 oz.) can refried beans
2 tsp. dried oregano
1 tsp. ground cumin
3/4 tsp. garlic powder
1 tsp. salt
12 uncooked lasagna noodles
2 1/2 c. water
2 1/2 c. salsa
2 c. sour cream
3/4 c. finely-sliced green onions
1 sm. can sliced black olives
1/2 c. grated cheese

Combine beef, beans, oregano, cumin and garlic powder. Place 4 of the noodles in bottom of 9x13-inch baking pan. Spread 1/2 of the beef mixture over them. Top with 4 more noodles and remaining beef mixture. Cover with last 4 noodles. Combine water and salsa. Pour over all. Cover with foil. Bake at 350° for 1 1/2 hours, or until noodles are tender. Combine sour cream, onions and olives. Spoon over and top with cheese. Bake, uncovered, until cheese is melted.

Marian Kasowski

Microwave Orange Roughy

1 Reynolds Oven Bag, large size (14"x20")
1 T. flour
4 orange roughy fillets (6 oz. each)
1 lg. tomato, chopped
1/4 c. chopped fresh basil or 1 tsp. dried basil
1/4 c. sliced green onion
2 cloves garlic, pressed
1/3 c. freshly-grated Parmesan cheese

Shake flour in Reynolds Oven Bag; place in 9x13x2-inch microwave-safe baking dish. Add orange roughy fillets to oven bag. Sprinkle fish with tomato, basil, green onion and garlic. Close oven bag with nylon tie; cut six 1/2-inch slits in top. Microwave on HIGH for 5 to 6 minutes for fresh fish or until fish flakes easily with a fork (13 to 14 minutes for frozen fish), turning dish halfway through cooking time. Let stand in oven bag 1 minute. Sprinkle with Parmesan cheese and let stand 1 minute longer before serving. Yield: 4 servings.

Reynolds Oven Bags Label

Minted Meat Balls

1 lb. lean ground beef
1 egg, beaten
1/2 c. finely-chopped onion
1 1/2 c. bread crumbs
3 T. lemon juice
2 T. chopped fresh mint
2 garlic cloves, pressed
Salt & pepper

MINTED YOGURT SAUCE:
8 oz. plain yogurt
3 T. chopped fresh mint
3 chopped green onions
1 garlic clove, pressed

Mix together few hours before serving and serve cool (not cold).

Combine all ingredients for meat balls. Form into small meat balls. Bake at 375° for 30 to 40 minutes, turning a couple of times to brown all sides. Serve with the Minted Yogurt Sauce using toothpicks to dip meat into sauce.

Debbi Grieco

Nancy's Corn, Cheese, Green Chili Pie

3 eggs
1 (8 oz.) can cream-style corn
1 (8 oz.) can whole kernel
  corn, drained
1 c. sour cream
4 oz. sharp Cheddar cheese
  (1 c.)
4 oz. Monterey Jack cheese
  (1 c.)
1 (4 oz.) can green chilies,
  drained, rinsed & chopped
1/2 c. yellow cornmeal
2 T. butter, melted
1 tsp. salt
1/4 tsp. Worcestershire sauce
Pinch of ground red pepper

Preheat oven to 350°. Grease 9x9x2-inch baking pan or 9-inch deep round baking pan. Beat eggs slightly in large bowl. Add cream-style corn and corn kernels, sour cream, cheese, green chilies, cornmeal, butter, salt, Worcestershire sauce and red pepper. Stir until well blended. Pour into prepared pan. Bake at 350° for 30 to 45 minutes, or until center is almost set. Remove pie to wire rack to cool slightly.
Serve with green salad and garlic toast.

Lila Hutchinson

No-Peel Potato Casserole

1 c. hot water
1 pkg. Lipton onion soup mix
1 stick margarine, melted
Pepper
8 (or more) unpeeled potatoes,
  cut 1/2" cubes (red potato
  best)
Parsley flakes

Combine water, soup mix, margarine and pepper. Mix and add potatoes in 2-quart greased casserole. Bake, covered, at 350° for 1 1/2 hours, or until done. Stir occasionally. Uncover last 30 minutes. Yield: 8 servings.

Donna Dewald

Oatmeal Meat Loaf

1 lb. ground round steak
1 egg, slightly beaten
2 T. chopped onion
1/2 c. coarse cracker crumbs
1 tsp. salt
2 T. melted butter
1/4 tsp. pepper
1/2 c. uncooked oatmeal
1 c. milk
2 slices bacon

Combine all ingredients except bacon. Form in loaf, lay bacon across top. Bake in moderate oven for 2 hours. Serve with tomato sauce.
For Kay!

Albert Hinrichs,
From: 1950 St. Paul's Lutheran Ladies Aid Cookbook

Pantry Pasta*

1 lb. dry pasta (any type)
2 (15 oz.) cans tomato sauce
1 (15 oz.) can diced tomatoes
1 tsp. basil (dry)
1/2 tsp. oregano (dry)
1/2 tsp. garlic salt
1/4 tsp. ground cayenne pepper
Parmesan cheese, grated, for garnish

Bring 5 quarts of water to a boil in a large pot. While water is heating, combine remaining ingredients in a saucepan and simmer. Prepare pasta according to package directions. Drain pasta and put back in large pot. Add sauce and mix together. Garnish with Parmesan cheese. Yield: 6 to 8 servings.

Total cooking time: about 20 minutes.

Variation: Ground beef, cubed chicken or pork can also be added. Cook meat in the saucepan before adding tomato sauces and spices.

Meridee Erickson-Stowman

Peasant-Style Chicken

6 chicken breasts, skinned
12 new potatoes, cut into halves
2 carrots, coarsely chopped
2 turnips, coarsely chopped
2 stalks celery, coarsely
3 c. red or white wine
1/4 c. olive oil
Salt & pepper, to taste
Mixture of 3 herbs such as: oregano, thyme, basil, tarragon, rosemary or dill, to taste

Rinse chicken and pat dry; place in deep baking dish. Add potatoes, carrots, turnips and celery. Combine wine, olive oil and seasonings in bowl; mix well. Pour over chicken and vegetables. Bake at 375° for 50 minutes, or until tender. Yield: 6 servings.

June Kaeding

Pheasant (Chicken) Dumpling Soup

Cover pheasant with water, boil until tender. Remove from broth and cut bird into pieces.

Add:

- 5 carrots, cut into 1/4" slices
- 1 med. onion, cut into pieces
- 2 T. chicken flavor stock granules
- 4 lg. stalks celery (use leaves)
- 3 to 4 cloves garlic

Boil until carrots are tender-crisp, adding water to cover. Then add 1/2 package frozen cut beans, peas and corn. Bring to boil.

DUMPLINGS:
- 2 eggs (whisk until blended)
- 1/2 c. water
- 1/2 tsp. salt
- Flour

Add salt, water and flour until thick to eggs. Drop into boiling soup with teaspoon (1/4 to 1/2 teaspoonful). Boil about 10 minutes until dumplings are cooked. Simmer until soup is served.

Helen Beyer

Pizza Meat Loaf*

- 2 lb. ground beef
- 1 c. cracker crumbs
- 1/2 c. chopped onion
- 2 eggs
- 1/2 c. Parmesan cheese
- 1 1/2 tsp. salt
- 1 tsp. oregano
- 1 c. milk

Mix together and bake 1 hour at 350°. Remove from oven, drain off grease and cover with:

- 1 (10 1/2 oz.) can pizza sauce
- 1 c. Mozzarella cheese

Return to oven for another 10 to 15 minutes.

Nancy Thiel

Pizza Casserole*

1 lb. ground beef
1 med. onion
Salt & pepper, to taste
1 can cream of mushroom soup
1 can tomato soup
1 c. Minute Rice
1/4 tsp. thyme
1/4 tsp. oregano
1/4 tsp. garlic powder
Grated cheese, any kind

Brown ground beef and onion. Add salt and pepper to taste. In separate saucepan, mix soup, seasonings and rice. Let simmer for 5 minutes. Combine two mixtures, pour into casserole dish and top with grated cheese. Bake at 350° for 30 minutes, or until cheese is golden and bubbly on top.

Doris Goberville

Pork Chop Ramen*

1 pkg. pork Ramen noodles
1/2 tsp. oil
2 pork chops
1/4 onion, sliced
1/2 can cream of celery soup
1/4 c. water

Cook noodles and drain. Add seasoning packet. Over medium heat, brown chops on both sides in oil for about 10 minutes. Drain fat. Add onion, soup concentrate and water. Simmer on low heat for 10 minutes. Serve on noodles.

Toni Patrick,
From: 101 Ways To Make Ramen Noodles

Potato Boats*

5 baked potatoes, sliced
  1/4" thick
3/4 c. salsa
1/2 c. shredded Cheddar cheese
3 T. bacon bits

Layer potatoes in a single layer on cookie sheet. Mix the salsa, cheese and bacon bits. Spoon cheese mixture onto potato slices. Bake at 425° for 15 minutes. Serve with sour cream.

Ryan Jonasson,
From: Heitkamp Family recipes

Potato Pepperoni Hot Dish*

1 1/2 to 2 lb. hamburger
1 can Cheddar cheese soup
1 can tomato soup
1 c. milk
1/2 tsp. oregano
1/4 tsp. pepper
1/2 c. Parmesan cheese
1 tsp. sugar
1 pkg. pepperoni
6 to 8 potatoes
1 sm. onion
1 c. Mozzarella cheese

Brown hamburger and onion. Mix soups, milk and seasoning. Mix together hamburger, potatoes and soup mixture. Place in 9x13-inch pan. Bake at 350° for 1 hour, or until potatoes are tender. Top with pepperoni slices. Bake for 5 minutes. Top with cheeses. Bake until cheese melts.

Rhonda Nudell

Quick Cabbage Soup*

1/4 c. instant minced onion
2 T. butter
3 c. cabbage, chopped
3 c. water
1 T. salt
2 c. potatoes, diced
1 (14 1/2 oz.) can evaporated milk

Cook potatoes and cabbage in salt water 15 to 20 minutes. (I prefer real onions, yellow – cook with cabbage and potatoes.) Add milk and butter and reheat. Do not boil. Sprinkle with minced parsley. Can add bits of ham or bacon.
Do not drain water.
Can omit potatoes.
Very easy.

Donna Johnson

Quick-Into-The-Oven Casserole*

1 lg. ham steak slice
1 (29 oz.) can cut sweet potatoes
2 lg. baking apples

Cut ham slice into serving pieces. Drain sweet potatoes, reserving syrup. Peel apples and slice. Arrange sweet potatoes in greased casserole dish. Top with apples. Place ham slices over apples and sweet potatoes. Pour some of the reserved syrup over all. Cover bottom of casserole with 1-inch or more of syrup. Cover and bake at 350° for 25 to 30 minutes, until apples are cooked. Serve with tossed green salad.
Keep these 3 key ingredients on hand for a quick, easy meal.

Carolyn Jolstad

Quick Pork Chops Over Stuffing*

2 (6 oz.) pkg. instant stuffing
   mix
3 1/3 c. chicken broth
1/2 c. butter

8 boneless pork loin chops
   (1/2" to 3/4" thick)
Worcestershire sauce (opt.)
Minced fresh parsley (opt.)

In a large saucepan, combine the vegetable/seasoning packets from stuffing mix with broth and butter. Bring to a boil. Reduce heat; cover and simmer for 5 minutes. Stir in stuffing. Cover and remove from the heat; let stand for 5 minutes. Spoon stuffing into eight mounds in a greased 9x13x2-inch baking dish. Place a pork chop over each mound. Sprinkle with Worcestershire sauce, if desired. Cover and bake at 425° for 15 minutes. Uncover; bake 20 minutes longer, or until meat juices run clear. Garnish with parsley, if desired. Yield: 8 servings.

From: Taste of Home

Ranch Potatoes*

2 lb. red potatoes, peeled &
   quartered
1 env. buttermilk dry salad
   dressing mix

1 (8 oz.) pkg. cream cheese
1 can cream of potato or cream
   of celery soup

Place potatoes in crock-pot. Combine rest of ingredients together and pour over potatoes. Cook 7 to 9 hours on low, 3 to 4 hours on high.

Joan Halland

Randy's Chili

1 lb. Louis Rich ground turkey
   (sold in a tube in the frozen
   foods section)
2 (16 oz.) cans dark red
   kidney beans
1 (10.5 oz.) can Campbell's
   tomato soup

1 (14.5 oz.) can stewed
   tomatoes
1 (14.5 oz.) can diced tomatoes
1 pkg. McCormick's mild chili
   seasoning
1 lg. white onion (or 2 med.-
   sized ones)

Thaw turkey overnight in refrigerator. In a 12- to 14-inch chef's pan or deep skillet: chop onion and brown together with turkey. Use spatula to chop turkey into small pieces. Brown until liquid from turkey is gone and onions are "clear". Add all remaining ingredients. At least one of the cans of kidney beans should be undrained to provide additional liquid to thin out the condensed tomato soup. Bring to a bubble, then reduce heat and continue cooking for 10 to 15 minutes. The skins on the kidney beans should <u>not</u> split. If they do, you are cooking too long.

This chili tastes best if left in the refrigerator overnight for the flavors to "marry", and then reheated.

Randy Burg

Rasta Pasta*

1 (8 oz.) box bow-tie pasta
1 tsp. chopped garlic
2 T. olive oil
1 c. chopped spinach, fresh
1 c. broccoli flowerets
1 med. red pepper, roasted & chopped
1 c. cut-up grilled chicken breast
1 c. prepared alfredo sauce (I used Ragu roasted garlic Parmesan cheese creation)
1/8 c. prepared basil pesto (I used Knorr pesto sauce)
1 tsp. Italian seasoning
2 T. shredded fresh Parmesan cheese

Cook pasta according to directions. Drain well; set aside. In 10-inch sauté pan, cook garlic in olive oil. Add spinach, broccoli, red pepper and chicken; toss to combine. Stir in alfredo sauce and pesto; simmer 5 minutes more. Reheat pasta if necessary under hot running water, drain. Put into bowl. Pour alfredo sauce mixture over bow-tie pasta. Sprinkle with Italian seasoning and Parmesan cheese.
Enjoy!

Colleen Clancy,
From: RainforestCafe.com

Roadside Potatoes*

3 c. half & half (cream)
1/2 c. butter
1 tsp. salt
2 (12 oz.) pkg. frozen hash browned, thawed
1/2 c. grated Parmesan cheese

Heat cream and butter just to boiling. Add salt. Place potatoes in thin layer in oblong baking dish (9x13-inches). Pour cream mixture over potatoes. Bake at 325° for 1 hour. Yield: 8 servings.

Jean Leaf

Russian River Chicken

1 (3 to 4 lb.) bird chicken
1 head garlic
4 sprigs fresh rosemary

Salt & pepper
Butter
Olive oil

Preheat oven to 375°. Wash chicken and remove anything inside (neck, giblets, etc.), including extra fat blob. Set chicken aside.

You need a roasting rack, cheap one it folds up and holds the bird aloft and it needs to fit into a roasting pan, place bird on rack and place rack into pan. Wash rosemary sprig and insert under the skin at breast (stick your finger in first to separate shin from meat and insert sprig on left side of breast) throw leftover rosemary into bird cavity. Take whole garlic head and cut the whole head in half so you have 2 heads of garlic with meat exposed, take one-half and throw it into cavity of bird. Take other half and remove two half cloves and peel and slice into pieces; insert under the other side of breast sooo now you have one side with garlic and the other with rosemary. Take slice of butter and throw into the bird cavity and also insert a little butter under skin with rosemary and garlic. Take a little bit of olive oil and rub bird. Now salt and pepper bird.

Add about 1/2-inch of water in pan and one chicken bouillon cube (break it up), you can get them anywhere they come in a small box. Insert the whole thing into the oven. Overall cooking time about one hour for 4 pound bird so don't forget to check it's weight before cooking, 3 pound bird about 55 minutes. After 15 minutes, take a baster and suck up some water from pan and baste bird, repeat every 10 to 15 minutes. <u>Add water every time you baste so the pan does not dry up – this is crucial.</u> A foolproof way to know when the bird is done is to grab a drumstick and shake it; if it's loose then the bird is done, if it seems rigid it needs more time…overall you should not cook the bird longer than 1 hour 15 minutes. Remove bird from rack and let it rest about 3 to 7 minutes, take pan and put on stove-top. Remove bird, put roasting pan on burner and simmer juices; add about a two tablespoons flour and whisk until thick.

Buy your chicken from a Chinese market – they are the best the ones. Do not buy from organic food store, not tasty. Always smell your bird when you get home, if it smells funny at all then it's no good – it happens more with the organics, than the Chinatown variety. <u>Don't get a bird over 4.5 pounds.</u> Sometimes I will take the neck if the bird comes with one and throw it in the roasting pan with the water and add extra flavor, just toss it when you start your gravy.

Ron Rodrigues,
Tom Lopez

Salisbury Steak*

1 1/2 lb. ground beef or bison
1 c. packaged stuffing mix
1 egg, beaten
Chopped onion, to taste
Salt & pepper
1 can beefy mushroom soup

Mix first five ingredients together. Form into patties and brown. Place in a baking dish. Cover with soup. Bake for 1 hour, baste after 30 minutes. Serve.
Freezes well.

Lois Berndt

Sauerkraut Casserole*

1 3/4 lb. ground beef
1 (27 oz.) can sauerkraut
1 (1 oz.) pkg. onion soup mix
1/2 c. uncooked rice
1 (10 3/4 oz.) can cream of mushroom soup
1 soup can water

Preheat oven to 350°. Brown ground beef; drain. Combine ground beef, drained sauerkraut, soup mix, rice, soup and water in bowl. Turn into 3-quart baking dish or casserole. Bake for 40 minutes, or until done. Yield: 8 servings.

Linda Jo Langemo

Scalloped Potatoes*

1 can whole kernel corn, drained
1 can cream of mushroom soup
3 c. milk
3 1/2 c. thinly-sliced white potatoes
Salt & pepper, to taste

Stir everything together. Put ingredients in large mixing bowl (microwave-safe). Add pats of butter to the top, cover. Microwave for about 17 to 19 minutes, turning and stirring after about 10 minutes. Remove and let stand 2 minutes before serving. Yield: 4 to 6 servings.
Total time: about 27 minutes.

Marcy Rynestad

Seafood Casserole*

1/4 lb. crabmeat, flaked
1/4 lb. shrimp
1/4 lb. scallops
1 can Cheddar cheese soup

Mix fish ingredients and place in greased casserole dish. Cover with soup and bake for 30 minutes at 400°. Serve with rice. Yield: 4 servings.
Very good!

Sandra Franke

Seafood Jubilee*

1 can tuna
1 can shrimp (or use fresh)
1 can mushroom soup
1 (4 oz.) can mushrooms
3/4 c. cream
3 oz. slivered almonds
1 c. cheese-flavored crackers, crushed
1 T. lemon juice
1 T. sherry
1 T. onion juice
1 c. ripe olives, sliced
1 c. frozen peas
Water chestnuts (opt.)

Mix all together in 2-quart casserole. Bake at 375° for 40 to 45 minutes, until hot and bubbly!

Joyce Johnson

Simple Chicken*

6 chicken breasts or thighs
1 can cream of mushroom soup
1 generous c. grated Cheddar cheese
1 bunch green onions, chopped
1 tsp. sage
Salt & pepper

Arrange chicken in a shallow 9x13-inch pan, skin-side up. Sprinkle with salt and pepper. Mix soup, cheese, onions and sage in a bowl. Spread over chicken. Bake at 400° for about 55 minutes, basting if necessary. Yield: 6 servings.

Kim Kusler

Skillet Barbecued Pork Chops*

1/3 c. honey
1/3 c. Italian dressing
4 boneless pork chops, 1/2" thick (about 1 lb.)
1/3 c. barbecue sauce
1 tsp. chili powder

In a large resealable plastic storage bag, combine the honey, barbecue sauce, Italian dressing and chili powder; mix well. Add the pork chops to the marinade; seal bag, shake to coat the meat well, then refrigerate for 1 hour. In a large skillet, cook the pork chops with the sauce mixture over medium-high heat for 3 to 4 minutes per side, or until no pink remains. Serve topped with the sauce.

From: Mr. Food – KVLY, Fargo

Sloppy Joes

1 1/2 lb. lean ground beef
1 sm. onion, minced
2 stalks celery, minced
1 (12 oz.) btl. chili sauce
2 T. brown sugar
1 T. Worcestershire sauce
1 tsp. salt
2 T. sweet pickle relish
1/8 tsp. pepper

In large skillet or slow-cooking pot with browning unit, cook beef with onion and celery until meat loses its red color. Pour off fat. In slow-cooking pot, combine meat, onion and celery with remaining ingredients. Cover and cook on low for 3 to 4 hours. Spoon over toasted hamburger buns or French rolls. Yield: 4 to 6 servings.

Laura Schock

Slow-Cooker Winter Vegetable Soup

1 lb. ground beef, browned & drained
1 (16 oz.) can stewed tomatoes
1 (15 oz.) can tomato sauce
1 pkg. dry onion soup mix
1 can beef broth
1 can water
1 pkg. frozen mixed vegetables

Mix all above ingredients together in slow-cooker and cook on low 7 to 9 hours. Yield: 10 servings.

Melva Glemming

Souper Enchiladas

1 pt. sour cream
2 cans cream of chicken soup
1 med. onion, chopped
1 pkg. lg. tortillas
2 (4 oz.) cans chopped green chilies
1 lb. Cheddar cheese
1 lb. hamburger, browned

Heat until bubbly: sour cream, green chilies and cream of chicken soup. Grate Cheddar cheese; add all but 1/4 cup to onion and mix with hamburger. Roll mixture into tortillas. Put a cup of soup mixture in bottom of 9x13-inch pan. Put tortillas on top. Pour rest of sauce over tortillas and top with grated cheese. Bake for 20 minutes at 350°.
Variation: Can use chicken instead of beef.
Works well in crock-pot on low 6 to 8 hours.

Sara Zaun

Speedy Rice Krispie Hot Dish*

1 can cream of chicken soup
1 can chicken with rice soup
1 lb. ground beef
4 c. Rice Krispies

Brown meat with onions, salt and pepper. Then add the soups, stir in Rice Krispies. Place in greased casserole. Bake for 30 minutes at 350°.

Gerry Hemberger,
From: Halstad, Mn. Community Cookbook

Supreme Lasagna

1 (1 lb.) pkg. lasagna noodles, uncooked
1 lb. ground beef
1/2 c. onion, chopped
1/4 tsp. garlic powder
1 1/2 tsp. salt
1/4 tsp. pepper
1/4 tsp. oregano
1/2 c. Parmesan cheese, divided
1 (28 oz.) can tomatoes
1 (8 oz.) can tomato sauce
3/4 lb. Mozzarella cheese
1 lb. cottage cheese or sour cream

Prepare noodles according to directions. Brown ground beef with onion. Add spices, 2 tablespoons Parmesan cheese, tomatoes and tomato sauce. Simmer 20 minutes. Layer alternately in 9x13-inch cake pan in this order: 1/3 meat sauce, 1/2 of the noodles, 1/2 of Mozzarella cheese, and cottage cheese, 2 tablespoons Parmesan cheese. Repeat layers. Bake at 350° for 30 minutes.

Dagmar Janish

Surprise Cheese Burgers

1 lb. ground beef
1/4 c. onions, minced
1 1/2 tsp. salt
1/4 tsp. pepper
1/8 tsp. onion salt
1/8 tsp. garlic salt
1/2 c. water
1 c. Cheddar cheese, shredded

DOUGH:
1 pkg. yeast
1 c. warm water
3 T. salad oil
3 T. sugar
1 tsp. salt
3 c. flour

Brown beef and onions together, then add salt, pepper, onion salt, garlic salt and water. Simmer about 10 minutes.

Dough: Combine yeast and water to dissolve. Then add oil, sugar and salt to yeast. Stir in flour to make a soft dough. Knead well until smooth and elastic. Divide into 12 portions. Cover and let rise for 5 minutes. Roll each into 5-inch rounds.

Spoon approximately 1/4 cup of meat and 2 to 3 tablespoons cheese on each round. Fold dough over filling and pinch edges to seal. Place seam-side down on greased baking sheet. Bake at 350° for 20 to 25 minutes, or until browned. Brush with melted butter, if desired, or serve with brown gravy.

Laura Schock

Taco Soup

1 lg. can tomato sauce
1 can crushed tomatoes
2 cans corn, with water
1 can pinto beans
2 lb. hamburger
2 pouches taco seasoning
2 med. onions, diced
2 c. water

Brown hamburger and onion; drain off grease and rinse. Add taco seasoning to hamburger and onion; pour into crock-pot. Add tomato sauce, crushed tomatoes, drained pinto beans and corn (do not drain corn). Add 2 cups water. Cook in crock-pot on low heat 4 to 6 hours, stirring occasionally. Serve with chopped black olives, sour cream, shredded cheese, chopped tomatoes for garnish and tortilla chips.

Andrea Richman

Tasty BBQ Pork Chops*

8 pork chops (with fat removed from edges)
4 T. vinegar
1/2 c. water
2/3 c. ketchup
1 med. onion, chopped
1/2 tsp. salt
2/3 c. brown sugar

Place chops in ungreased 9x13-inch pan. Mix all other ingredients and pour over chops. Bake, uncovered, at 350° for 1 hour and 15 minutes.

Pat Buerkle

Teriyaki Pork Roast

3/4 c. unsweetened apple juice
2 T. sugar
2 T. soy sauce
1 T. vinegar
1 tsp. ground ginger
1/4 tsp. garlic powder
1/8 tsp. pepper
1 boneless pork roast (about 3 lb.)
7 1/2 tsp. cornstarch
3 T. cold water

Combine the first 7 ingredients in a greased slow-cooker. Add roast and turn to coat. Cover and cook on low for 7 to 8 hours, or until a thermometer inserted in roast reads 160°. Remove roast and keep warm. Combine cornstarch and water, stir into cooking juices. Bring to boil; cook and stir for 2 minutes. Serve with roast. Yield: 8 servings.

Pauline Lentz

Better to suffer for the truth than be praised for a lie.
Swedish proverb

Teriyaki Salmon with Red Potatoes

I recommend serving with lightly steamed asparagus, fresh bread and a buttery California North Coast Chardonnay.

10 to 14 oz. salmon steak (**important** – steak, not fillet)	Red potatoes
Teriyaki sauce (I highly recommend a produced called Veri teriyaki by Soy Vay, Felton, CA – www.soyvay.com 800-600-2077)	Olive oil Minced garlic

Rinse off salmon under cold running water. Place salmon in bowl of teriyaki sauce, about 3/4 of height of the fish. Cover in plastic shrink-wrap and leave in the refrigerator all day. About an hour before cooking, flip it over and put back in the refrigerator. Broil for 11 to 14 minutes, but keep a close watch as all ovens vary.

Add a dash of kosher salt and olive oil to a pot of water, put potatoes in the boiling water and cook for 12 to 18 minutes (depending on the size of the potatoes). To see if they are done, stick them with a fork, if it slides in easy, they are done. Mix a little olive oil with minced garlic, lightly brush over the top of the potatoes, add salt and pepper.

Tom Lopez

Tina's Cheesy Potato Bake*

1 can cream of chicken soup	2 c. Cheddar cheese
12 oz. sour cream	2 c. corn flakes
1 (2 lb.) bag frozen hash brown potatoes	1/2 c. melted butter (1/4 c. mixed in, 1/4 c. on top)
1/2 tsp. salt	

Mix all ingredients; add butter on top. Bake for 1 hour at 350°.

Really quick to make. Double the recipe for big family gatherings. Super potato dish served with ham.

Tina Tungseth

Tortellini and Bean Soup*

3 T. olive oil
1 med. onion, chopped
1 garlic clove, crushed
1 c. canned chopped tomatoes, drained
8 c. low-salt chicken broth
1 tsp. dried oregano
1 tsp. dried basil
3 (15 oz.) cans black beans, rinsed & drained
2 T. rice vinegar
Black pepper, to taste
12 oz. fresh or frozen tortellini

In a large soup pot, heat the olive oil over medium heat. Add the onion and sauté for 3 minutes. Add the garlic and drained tomatoes; cook for 3 minutes. Add the chicken broth, oregano, basil, drained black beans, vinegar and black pepper. Reduce the heat to low and simmer for 5 minutes. Finally, add the tortellini to the soup and cook for 8 minutes, or until tender. Yield: 8 servings.

Laura Schock

Tortilla Soup

1 to 1 1/2 lb. ground beef
1 sm. onion, chopped
1 (28 oz.) can diced tomatoes
1 (10 oz.) can Ro-Tel (tomatoes & green chilies)
1 (15 oz.) can corn
2 (15 oz.) cans beans: kidney, navy, pinto or Great Northern
1 can beer
1 pkg. dry taco seasoning
1 pkg. dry Hidden Valley Ranch dressing mix

Brown ground beef with onion; drain off excess fat. Into a large soup pot, open and pour <u>entire</u> contents of every can. Add taco seasoning and dry dressing mix. Add ground beef/onion mixture; stir, mixing all ingredients thoroughly. Simmer for an hour or so. Serve topped with grated Cheddar cheese and dollop of sour cream. Add tortilla chips and/or cornbread as "sides" when serving. Yield: 8 to 10 servings.

This tastes even better the next day!

Nela Glemming

He who would harvest honey must endure the sting of bees.
Swedish proverb

Turkey Burgers*

1 lb. ground turkey (white meat preferred)
1 lg. clove garlic, diced or pressed
1 T. chopped chives or onion
1/3 c. Parmesan cheese, grated
1/4 tsp. pepper
1/8 tsp. salt (opt.)

Mix all ingredients together. Form into 1/4 pound patties (or smaller). Spray a plate with cooking spray. Add a bit of cooking oil to the tops of the patties. Then spray the other side of patties when you move them to the plate. Grill or fry on medium heat. Do not overcook. Serve on buns with barbecue sauce, sautéed onions and/or sliced tomatoes.
Very tasty!
We use ground turkey breast – so they are low-fat.
I oil my hands lightly to make the turkey easier to work with.

Joyce Baldwin

Turkey Sausage*

1 lb. ground turkey
1/2 tsp. crushed dried red pepper
1/2 tsp. fennel
1/2 tsp. rosemary
1/2 tsp. poultry seasoning mix
Salt & pepper, to taste

Stir spices together, then sprinkle over ground turkey and mix thoroughly. Shape into patties and fry, uncover. A frypan works well.
Or: brown and crumble like hamburger. Stir in 1 can mushroom soup and 1/2 can milk. Heat through. Serve over biscuits or potatoes.

Deb Tuck

Tuscan White Bean Soup*

2 tsp. olive oil
1 c. chopped ham
1 c. chopped onion
3/4 c. chopped celery
1 garlic clove, minced
1 can fat-free chicken broth
2 (19 oz.) cans undrained cannellini or other white beans
2 bay leaves
2 T. minced parsley
1/4 tsp. pepper
2 T. sherry (opt.)

Heat oil, add celery, carrots, onions and garlic. Sauté for 2 minutes. Add ham and sauté until vegetables are soft, using low heat. Add water, beans, bay leaves and broth. Bring to a boil, reduce heat, partially cover kettle and simmer 25 to 30 minutes. Add parsley, pepper and sherry. Discard bay leaves and serve.
Add a green salad and toasted Italian bread. A tasty low-fat meal.

Doris Sauerland

X-Tra Good Vegetable Soup

1 env. Mrs. Grass' vegetable soup mix
4 T. dried vegetable flakes
Dash of garlic salt
Dash of sage
Dash of Nature's seasonings
Dash of Italian seasoning
Dash of chili powder
5 beef bouillon cubes, dissolved in 5 c. very hot water
2 c. chopped carrots
1/2 c. chopped rutabaga
2 c. chopped cabbage (coleslaw mix works well)
1 lb. stew meat (small pieces seasoned with salt & pepper, browned)
1/2 c. chopped onion
4 chopped potatoes

Best when simmered in a crock-pot all day, even better the next day.

Roger Hovelson via Bette Hovelson

Notes & Recipes

Fuel Stop - Cookies & Bars

Notes & Recipes

Fuel Stop – Cookies & Bars

Almond Cookies*

Sift onto a piece of waxed paper and set aside:
- 3 c. sifted flour
- 1/2 tsp. salt
- 1 tsp. baking soda

Cream:
- 1 c. vegetable shortening
- 1/2 c. butter

Add:
- 1 c. sugar
- 1 tsp. almond extract
- 1 egg

Mix thoroughly and then gradually add dry ingredients. Roll into 1-inch balls and place onto greased cookie sheet. Make an indentation in center of each ball and place in it: a blanched almond or 1/2 of a drained maraschino cherry or 1/4 teaspoon seedless jam or jelly.

Valerie Snebold,
From: San Francisco Chronicle, 1969

Every cake seeks its match.
Swedish proverb

Almond-Glazed Sugar Cookies*

1 c. Land O' Lakes soft baking butter with canola oil
3/4 c. sugar
1 tsp. almond extract

2 c. all-purpose flour
1/2 tsp. baking powder
1/4 tsp. salt

GLAZE:
1 1/2 c. powdered sugar
1 tsp. almond extract

4 to 5 tsp. water
Sliced almonds

Heat oven to 400°. Combine first 3 cookie ingredients in large mixer bowl. Beat at medium speed, scraping bowl often, until creamy (1 to 2 minutes). Reduce speed to low; add all remaining cookie ingredients. Beat until well mixed.

Roll dough into 1-inch balls. Place 2 inches apart onto ungreased cookie sheets. Flatten balls to 1/4-inch thickness with bottom of buttered glass dipped in sugar. Bake for 7 to 9 minutes, or until edges are very lightly browned. Cool 1 minute; remove from cookie sheets. Cool completely.

Stir together all glaze ingredients, except almonds, with wire whisk in small bowl. Decorate cooled cookies with glaze and sliced almonds. Yield: 3 1/2 dozen cookies.

Preparation time: 30 minutes. Baking time: 7 minutes.

Tips: Glaze sets up quickly, so decorate a few cookies at a time. If dough is too dry, stir in 1 to 2 tablespoons milk.

Variations: Flavored: Substitute vanilla or mint flavoring for almond extract. Toppings: Drizzle unglazed cookies with melted chocolate or vanilla-flavored candy coating (almond bark). Decorate glazed cookies with chopped nuts, miniature chocolate chips or colored sugars.

Storage: Store cookies in a loosely-covered container for up to 1 week.

Marcella Richman,

From: Land O' Lakes butter

Everyday is a birthday; every moment of it is new to us; we are born again, renewed for fresh work and endeavor.
Isaac Watts

Best Brownies*

1 c. butter
1 c. sugar
4 eggs
1 tsp. vanilla

1 (16 oz.) can chocolate syrup
1 c. flour
1/2 tsp. baking powder

QUICK FROSTING:
1 c. sugar
1/4 c. milk

1/4 c. butter or margarine
1/2 c. chocolate chips

Cream butter and sugar. Beat in eggs. Add vanilla and chocolate syrup. Add flour with baking powder. Mix all well. Spread in 10x15-inch greased pan. Bake at 350° for 30 minutes.

Bring first 3 frosting ingredients to a boil. Remove from heat. Add chocolate chips. Stir. Spread over bars.

Carol Grindberg

Best Oatmeal Cookies*

6 eggs, beaten
1 lb. raisins
1/4 c. vanilla
1/4 c. cinnamon
1 c. shortening
1 c. margarine

2 c. white sugar
2 c. brown sugar
2 1/4 c. white flour
2 1/2 c. wheat flour
4 tsp. baking soda
4 c. oatmeal

Combine eggs, raisins, vanilla and cinnamon; let stand 1 to 2 hours. Cream sugars and shortening. Add other ingredients. Bake at 350°. Yield: 6 dozen.

Susan Martinez

Candy Cane Snowballs*

2 c. butter (no substitutes), softened
1 c. confectioners' sugar
1 tsp. vanilla
3 1/2 c. flour

1 c. pecans, chopped
8 oz. white candy coating (almond bark)
1/3 to 1/2 c. crushed peppermint candy

In a large mixing bowl, cream butter and sugar. Stir in vanilla. Gradually add flour. Stir in pecans. Refrigerate for 3 to 4 hours, or until easy to handle. Roll into 1-inch balls. Place 2 inches apart on ungreased baking sheets. Bake at 350° for 18 to 20 minutes, or until lightly browned. Remove to wire racks to cool.

In a microwave-safe bowl, melt candy coating; stir until smooth. Dip the top of each cookie into the candy coating, then into the peppermint candy. Yield: 5 dozen.

Marlys Freadhoff

Caramel-Nut Wedges*

1 refrigerated ready-to-bake pie crust (from a 15 oz. box of 2)
3/4 c. fat-free caramel ice cream topping
2 lg. eggs
2 T. stick butter, melted
1 tsp. vanilla extract
1 (10 oz.) can salted mixed nuts

Heat oven to 450°. Line a 9-inch round cake pan with foil, letting ends extend about 2 inches above pan.
Unfold pie crust in pan. Press into pan; fold edges down slightly to make a 1-inch high lip. Press edges gently with a fork, then prick crust with a fork. Press a sheet of foil snugly onto crust. Bake 12 minutes, remove top foil and bake 6 minutes more, until lightly browned. Reduce heat to 350° F.
Meanwhile, whisk ice cream topping, eggs, butter and vanilla in a medium bowl until well blended. Pour into crust; scatter nuts evenly over top.
Bake 25 to 30 minutes, until puffed, lightly browned and knife inserted near center comes out clean. Remove to a wire rack to cool. Refrigerate at least 4 hours to firm. Lift foil by ends to cutting board. Cut into 24 wedges.
From: Woman's Day, 9/16/03

Cashew Cookies*

1/2 c. butter
1 c. firmly-packed brown sugar
1 egg
1/2 tsp. vanilla
3/4 tsp. baking soda
3/4 tsp. baking powder
2 c. flour, sifted
1/3 c. sour cream
1 3/4 c. salted whole cashews

FROSTING:
1/2 c. butter
3 T. cream
1/4 tsp. vanilla
2 c. powdered sugar

Cream butter and sugar until fluffy. Add eggs and vanilla; mix well. Combine dry ingredients and add alternately with sour cream; mix well. Fold in cashews. Drop by teaspoonfuls on greased cookie sheet. Bake at 375° for 10 minutes. Cool. Frost.
Frosting: Brown butter slightly; remove from heat and add cream and vanilla. Stir in powdered sugar, and beat until smooth. Top with a cashew.
Linda Milbrandt

Carrot Bars*

4 eggs, beaten
2 tsp. baking soda
1 tsp. salt
2 1/2 c. flour

3 jars strained carrots (baby food)
2 c. sugar
2 tsp. cinnamon
1 1/2 c. Crisco oil

FROSTING:
3 1/2 c. powdered sugar
1 (8 oz.) pkg. soft cream cheese

1/2 c. butter
1 tsp. vanilla

Mix all ingredients together. Bake at 350° for 30 to 40 minutes in a jellyroll pan, 11x15 inches. Cool and then frost.
Frosting: Mix all frosting ingredients together. Beat and spread over cool bars.

Patty Trapp

Chocolate Chip Bars*

1 (18 1/2 oz.) pkg. yellow cake mix
1/2 c. oil

2 eggs
1 (12 oz.) pkg. semi-sweet chocolate chips

Preheat oven to 325°. In a large bowl, combine cake mix, oil and eggs. Mix by hand until well blended. Add chocolate chips; mix well. Pat into ungreased 10x15-inch jellyroll pan. Bake for 15 minutes (bars will be light golden, do not overbake). Yield: 30 to 40 bars.

Sonja Jorgensen

Chocolate-Chocolate Brownies*

1 prepackaged brownie mix (for 9"x13" pan)

1 (12 oz.) pkg. chocolate chips

Prepare prepackaged brownie mix as directed. Add chocolate chips. Bake according to brownie mix directions.
Very chocolaty! No need to frost! If one bag sounds like too much, reduce chocolate chips to your liking. Kids <u>love</u> them!

Jenni Richman

Chocolate Cookie Treats*

2 (8 oz.) Hershey's almond chocolate bars
4 to 5 c. corn flakes

Melt chocolate bars in top of a double boiler. Add corn flakes. Stir to coat flakes. Drop by teaspoon onto waxed paper. Cool and enjoy!
My family's favorite cookie.
So easy…and everyone wonders what they are made of!

Carolyn Jolstad

Chocolate-Peanut-Heath Cookie*

1 c. butter-flavor Crisco
1/2 c. white sugar
3/4 c. brown sugar
2 eggs
1 tsp. vanilla
2 1/4 c. flour
1 tsp. baking soda
1 tsp. salt
1/4 c. cocoa
1 c. chopped peanuts
1 (8 oz.) bag Heath bits

Cream Crisco and sugars. Add eggs and vanilla; mix well. Sift and add all dry ingredients. Mix in nuts and Heath bits. Form into 1-inch balls and press slightly with a fork on ungreased cookie sheet. Bake at 350° for 8 to 9 minutes; allow to cool a few minutes before removing from baking sheet. Yield: 3 to 4 dozen.

Dean Sauer

Time is a dressmaker specializing in alterations.
Faith Baldwin

Thick, Soft and Chewy Chocolate Chip Cookies*

1 1/4 c. all-purpose flour
1/2 tsp. baking soda
1/4 tsp. salt
1/2 c. (1/4 lb.) butter or margarine, at room temp.
3/4 c. brown sugar
1/2 tsp. vanilla
1 lg. egg
1 (6 oz.) pkg. semi-sweet chocolate chips
1/2 c. nuts (opt.)

Mix flour, baking soda and salt. Beat butter, sugar and vanilla with a mixer on medium speed until well blended. Beat in egg, mixing well. Add flour mixture and beat slowly to incorporate, then beat to blend well. Stir in chocolate chips and nuts. Drop batter into 2 tablespoon portions, about 2 inches apart on baking sheets. Bake in a 400° oven until edges of cookies are brown, but an area about 1-inch wide in the center is still pale…6 to 7 minutes. If using 2 pans in 1 oven, switch positions about half-time.

Let cookies cool on pan about 5 minutes, then transfer to racks with a spatula. Serve warm or cool. Store airtight up to 8 hours or freeze for longer storage. Yield: about 18 cookies…you will want to double this recipe, 18 is not enough!

Preparation time: about 10 minutes. Baking time: 7 minutes.

From: Sunset magazine

People don't know whether it is winter or summer when they are happy.
Anton Chekov

Thin, Crispy Chocolate Chip Cookies*

1 c. all-purpose flour
3/4 tsp. baking soda
1/4 tsp. salt
1/2 c. melted butter or margarine
1/2 c. firmly-packed brown sugar
1/3 c. granulated sugar
1/2 tsp. vanilla
1 (6 oz.) pkg. or 1 c. semi-sweet chocolate chips
1/2 c. chopped nuts (opt.)

Mix flour, baking soda and salt. With a mixer on medium speed, beat butter, brown sugar, granulated sugar, 3 tablespoons water and vanilla until blended. Stir flour mixture into butter mixture, then beat until blended. Stir in chocolate chips and nuts. Drop batter in 1 tablespoon portions about 2 inches apart in 300° oven until an even golden brown, 18 to 20 minutes. If using 2 pans, rotate positions. Remove from oven; let cookies cool on pan for about 3 minutes, then transfer to racks with a spatula. Serve warm or cool. Store airtight up to 1 day or freeze for longer storage. Yield: about 32 cookies.
Preparation time: about 10 minutes. Cooking time: 20 minutes.

What makes cookies chewy? High moisture content, stiffer dough, bigger amounts of dough per cookie, shorter baking time at higher temperature, NOT OVERBAKING. Remove from oven when outside of cookie is brown and at least 1/3 of center remains pale…the center remains soft.
What makes cookies crispy? Reducing the amount of ingredients that hold moisture: flour, eggs and brown sugar. Baking at lower temperature for longer time to brown and dry cookies.
What makes cookies spread: Most often it is using low-fat butter or margarine, which is about 20% water. Cookies also spread if you drop dough on hot baking sheets…the heat melts the dough and cookies spread before they are baked enough to hold their shape.

From: Sunset magazine

Pull out a gray hair and seven will come to its funeral.
Old Dutch saying

Coconut-Pecan Cookies*

1 c. butter, softened
3/4 c. sugar
3/4 c. brown sugar
2 eggs
1 tsp. vanilla

2 1/4 c. flour
1 tsp. baking soda
1 tsp. salt
4 c. chocolate chips, divided
1/4 c. coconut

FROSTING:
1 egg
1 (5 oz.) can evaporated milk
2/3 c. sugar

1/4 c. butter (no substitutes)
1 1/3 c. coconut
1/2 c. pecans

Frosting: In a saucepan, combine the egg, milk, sugar and butter. Cook and stir over medium heat for 10 to 12 minutes, or until slightly thickened and mixture reaches 160°. Stir in coconut and pecans; set aside.

In a mixing bowl, cream butter and sugars. Add eggs, one at a time, beating well after each addition. Beat in vanilla. Combine the flour, baking soda and salt. Gradually add to creamed mixture. Stir in 2 cups chocolate chips and coconut. Drop by tablespoonfuls 2 inches apart onto ungreased baking sheets. Bake at 350° for 8 to 10 minutes, until lightly browned. Cool 10 minutes before removing to wire racks; cool completely.

In microwave, melt the remaining chocolate chips. Stir until smooth. Frost cooled cookies. Drizzle with melted chocolate.

Marlys Freadhoff

Chocolate Pecan Shortbread Cookies*

1 c. butter, softened
3/4 c. brown sugar, packed
2 tsp. vanilla
2 c. flour

1/2 (10 oz.) pkg. Gurley's golden recipe chocolate almond bark
1 c. Gurley's golden recipe pecan halves, finely chopped

Preheat oven to 325°. In a large mixing bowl, cream together butter and sugar at medium speed. Add vanilla and flour; blend thoroughly at low speed. Shape level tablespoonfuls into balls and shape into logs 2 inches long and 1-inch wide. Place on ungreased cookie sheet 2 inches apart. Bake for 17 to 19 minutes, or until cookies spread and turn a light golden brown. Transfer immediately to a cool surface. Melt bark according to package directions. When cookies are completely cool, dip top third of cookie into warm bark, then into chopped pecans; place on waxed paper and refrigerate to set. Yield: 30 cookies.

Marcella Richman,
From: Gurley's golden recipe pecan halves

Cream Cheese Cookies*

1 (3 oz.) pkg. cream cheese
1 c. butter (not margarine)
2 c. flour
1/2 c. sugar
1 T. vanilla

Soften cream cheese and butter. Blend well. Combine flour and sugar. Add to butter mixture. Add vanilla and mix well. Shape into small balls and place on ungreased cookie sheet. Press chocolate chips or pecan halves into each cookie. Bake a t350° for 12 minutes until lightly browned. Yield: 5 to 6 dozen.

From: Tea Time at the Masters

Cream Cheese German Chocolate Cake Bars*

Grease and flour a jellyroll pan. Make a German chocolate cake as directed on box.
Beat together:

8 oz. cream cheese
1 egg
1/3 c. sugar
1 c. chocolate chips

Drop by teaspoon onto cake batter. Sprinkle on cake batter more chips and 1 cup chopped walnuts. Bake at 350° for 25 minutes.

Gladys Ratzlaff

Cute Christmas Cookie*

Round pretzels
Chocolate kisses
Red M&M's

Place a Hershey's kiss (unwrapped!) on a small, round pretzel. Melt slightly in a microwave. Top with a red M&M.
Pretty on Christmas cookie tray.

Lois Smith

Cut-Out Sugar Cookies*

Cream:
1 c. margarine
1 c. powdered sugar
1 tsp. vanilla
1 egg

2 1/2 c. flour
1/2 tsp. baking soda
1/2 tsp. cream of tartar

No need to chill dough, actually works better if dough isn't chilled. Roll out and cut with cookie cutter. Bake at 350° for 8 to 10 minutes.
  I usually double this recipe. Don't roll too thin or they can break as you frost the cookie.
  This is a great recipe!

Candy Odegaard

Date Cookies*

2 sticks margarine
2 c. light brown sugar
3 eggs
1 tsp. baking soda
1/4 tsp. salt

2 1/2 c. all-purpose flour
1 (10 oz.) ctn. diced, sugared dates
1 (10 oz.) pkg. chopped English walnuts

Preheat oven to 350°. Using an electric mixer, cream margarine. Add sugar, eggs, baking soda, salt and flour; mix well. Stir in dates and walnuts. Drop by teaspoonfuls on greased cookie sheet. Bake 10 to 12 minutes. Yield: 75 to 100 cookies.
  This recipe makes 4 dozen large cookies, or 100 bite-sized. Reserve some chopped dates and walnuts to place on top of each cookie before baking. This gives them a chunky and appetizing look.

Marilyn Decker

I'm not aging, I'm marinating.
seen on a T-shirt

Deluxe Chocolate-Marshmallow Bars*

3/4 c. butter
1 1/2 c. sugar
3 eggs
1 tsp. vanilla
1 1/3 c. flour

1/2 tsp. baking powder
3 T. cocoa
1/2 c. chopped nuts
1 pkg. or 4 c. marshmallows

TOPPING:
1 1/3 c. chocolate chips
3 T. butter

1 c. peanut butter
2 c. Rice Krispies

Preheat oven to 350°. Spray large bar pan with cooking oil.
Mix butter, sugar, eggs and vanilla. Beat until fluffy. Combine flour, baking powder, salt and cocoa; add to first mixture. Stir in nuts. Put in large pan, greased. Bake for 15 to 18 minutes. Do not overbake.
After baking, sprinkle the almonds evenly over the bars. Return to oven for 2 to 3 minutes longer. Use a knife dipped in water to spread marshmallows. Cool.
Combine chips, butter and peanut butter. Heat in a saucepan until mixture is smooth and well blended. (This could be done in the microwave, too; watch and stir until blended.) Remove from heat. Stir in cereal. Spread over bars. Yield: 3 dozen.

Mae Triebold

Drumsticks*

ROD PRETZELS:
1 bag caramels (at least 25 pieces)

Crushed peanuts, cashews, pecans

1 T. butter
2 T. milk

Chocolate almond bark
1/2 c. white chocolate chips;
1/2 c. milk chocolate chips

Melt bag of caramels with butter and milk. Melt chocolate almond bark with 1/2 cup milk chocolate chips and 1/2 cup white chocolate chips. Break rod pretzels in half. Dip broken end into caramel topping. Tap off. Roll in crushed nuts. Cool in refrigerator. Dip in melted almond bark and chips. Chill.

Colleen Clancy

Easy Coconut Brownies*

1 box Betty Crocker chocolate chunk family-size brownie mix*
2 eggs
1/4 c. butter
1/4 c. water
1 c. shredded coconut

Preheat oven to 350°. Grease a 9x13-inch baking pan. Mix half of the brownie mix with the other ingredients, then stir in the remaining mix. Pat into pan. Bake about 20 minutes. Brownies will shrink from the edge of the pan and still leave a crumb on a toothpick. Cool completely. Brownies are very delicate and not easy to get out of the pan.

*Pillsbury brownie mix does not give the same results at all. Have never tried Duncan Hines. Shortening does not give same result. Parchment paper might help with removal from pan, haven't tried it. They are so rich, we don't frost them.

For a cake-like brownie, use a chocolate cake mix (not one with syrup pouch). The brand doesn't seem to matter much here. The original recipe called for cake mix; Connie discovered it was much better with Betty Crocker brownie mix.

Kay and Connie Sauer

Favorite Dump Bars*

2 c. sugar
1 3/4 c. flour
5 eggs
1 tsp. salt
1 c. oil
1/2 c. cocoa
1 c. chocolate chips

Dump all ingredients together in a large bowl and mix together until ingredients are moist. Put into a 9x13-inch greased and floured pan. Bake at 350° for 20 to 25 minutes, but do not overbake. Are supposed to be moist.

Diane Kohler

Freckles*
(Pretty Fast Cookies)

1 pkg. Oreo cookies
8 oz. cream cheese
1 pkg. almond bark

Soften and beat cream cheese. Crumble or crush Oreo cookies (either with food processor or rolling pin – rolling cookies between 2 sheets of waxed paper).

Mix crushed cookies with softened cream cheese. Roll into walnut-sized balls. Place on cookie sheet and cool in refrigerator until firm. Melt almond bark. Dip cookies, one by one, in melted bark. Refrigerate. Can also drizzle with a bit of melted chocolate.

**Nancy Thiel,
Evelyn Jensen**

Haystacks*

4 Hershey's milk chocolate bars
1/2 c. raisins
2 c. Fiber One (cereal)

Measure Fiber One and raisins in bowl. Melt chocolate bars in microwave. Add melted chocolate to bowl with cereal and raisins. Mix well. Drop by heaping tablespoons onto waxed paper-covered cookie sheet. Cool in refrigerator or freezer until firm. Store in sealed container in refrigerator or freezer.
Tasty and healthy!
This is one of the many recipes I have received since joining Weight Watchers. It is possible to eat healthy and enjoy good food!

Carol Jendro

Joel's "One" Cookies*

1 c. sugar
1 (12 oz.) box corn flakes
1 c. light corn syrup
(about 8 c.)
1 c. creamy peanut butter

In a 5-quart saucepot, mix sugar and corn syrup; heat to boiling over high heat, stirring frequently. Boil 1 minute. Remove saucepot from heat and stir in peanut butter until blended. Add corn flakes, stirring gently to coat. Working quickly, drop mixture by 1/4 cups, 2 inches apart, on countertop lined with waxed paper or foil. Shape each cookie with fingers into a rounded mound if necessary. Let cookies stand 20 to 30 minutes at room temperature to set. Store cookies in tightly-covered container at room temperature. Yield: 24 cookies.
Preparation time: 10 minutes. Cooking time: 3 minutes.
Variation: Stir in 1/2 cup dried tart cherries or cranberries with the peanut butter.

*Joel Darrington,
From: Good Housekeeping*

Joe's Peanut Bars*

1 bag chocolate chips
1 bag milk chocolate chips
1 bag butterscotch chips
1 1/2 c. creamy peanut butter
1/2 c. butter
1/4 c. half & half or milk

Melt all ingredients together. In a large, buttered pan or a buttered cookie sheet, spread a layer of marshmallows (about 2 cups) and salted peanuts (2 cups). Next, spread the melted ingredients over. Using a spoon, lightly mix in the peanuts and the marshmallows. Refrigerate to firm up. Tastes like Peanut Buster Parfait!

Ann Richman Cease

Lemon Bars*
(With Spice Cake Apple Variation)

Lemon cake mix
Lemon pie filling
2 eggs

Mix and bake in a jellyroll pan. Frost the canned lemon frosting. Can use other cake mixes and pie filling flavors for other types of bars (spice cake mix with apple pie filling and 2 eggs for spice bars; frost with cream cheese frosting).

Tammy Buhr Erickson

Mixed Nut Bars*

1 1/2 c. flour
3/4 c. brown sugar
1/4 tsp. salt
1/3 c. margarine

Mix above like pie crust. Press into 9x13-inch pan. Bake at 350° for 10 minutes. Add 1 can mixed nuts on top.
Melt:

1 (6 oz.) pkg. butterscotch chips
1/2 c. white syrup
2 T. butter

Pour over nuts. Bake 10 minutes more.

LaVira Eggermont

Moist Brownies*

2 1/2 c. flour
2 c. sugar
1/2 c. sour cream
1 tsp. salt
1 tsp. baking soda

2 eggs
2 sticks margarine
5 T. cocoa powder
1 c. water

Preheat oven to 350°. In a large bowl, stir together flour, sugar, sour cream, salt, baking soda and eggs. Bring margarine, cocoa and water to a boil in a saucepan. Stir this into flour mixture until smooth. Pour into a greased and floured 11x20-inch jellyroll pan. Bake for 20 to 22 minutes.

FROSTING:
1 lb. powdered sugar
1/2 c. walnuts, well chopped
1 stick margarine

1 tsp. vanilla
3 T. cocoa powder
6 T. milk

Bring margarine, cocoa and milk to a boil in a medium-sized saucepan. Remove from heat. Add sugar, vanilla and nuts; stir until smooth. Frost evenly over cooled brownies.
Maxine McCarthy

Molasses Roll-Outs*

1 c. lard
1 c. sugar
2 c. molasses
1 tsp. cinnamon
1 heaping tsp. ginger

1/2 tsp. nutmeg
1 tsp. baking soda
1/2 tsp. salt
1 c. sour cream
Flour, to stiffen (about 12 c.)

This recipe takes a large bowl.
For peppernuts, leave out ginger and add 2 teaspoons pepper.
Mix all ingredients. Add flour until a nice consistency to roll. Roll out.
Makes great Christmas gingerbread men.

These cookies were made by Emma (Wegner) Buchholz, when she helped her sister cook for threshers in a cook car, before the turn of the 20th century. They are best made with real sour cream and lard. Now I use heavy cream from a carton. I only take out about 2 cups dough before I add the ginger; to the 2 cups, add pepper.

I've made these cookies for more than 50 years, but it's hard to explain the process.
Rhoda Huber

"Monies" Sand Bakkels*

2 c. butter
2 c. sugar
1 egg
1/2 c. almonds
1 tsp. almond flavoring
5 c. all-purpose flour

Cream shortening. Add sugar and cream well. Add egg and almond extract. Add flour to make a stiff dough. Pinch off small ball of dough. Place in center of sand bakkel tin. Press evenly on inside of tin with thumb, spreading as thin as possible. Bake at 350° for 15 minutes, or until golden brown. Cool before removing from pan.

To remove from tin: tip and tap gently. Clean tins with clean cloth only. Can be used for tarts, with filling, as lemon, chocolate, fruit, whipped cream or nuts.

Pr. Mary Wallum

Chewy Ginger Cookies*
(Motor Munchies)

3/4 c. shortening
1 1/4 c. sugar, divided
1/4 c. molasses
1 tsp. vanilla
2 c. all-purpose flour
1 tsp. ground cinnamon
1 tsp. ground ginger
1 tsp. baking soda
1/2 tsp. salt
1/2 tsp. ground cloves

In a mixing bowl, cream shortening and 1 cup sugar. Add the egg, molasses and vanilla; mix well. Combine dry ingredients; add to creamed mixture and mix well. Roll into 1-inch balls; roll in remaining sugar. Place 1 1/2 inches apart on ungreased baking sheets. Bake at 375° for 10 minutes, or until lightly browned. Cool on wire racks. Store in an airtight container. Yield: 4 dozen.

"Take-alongs" for a road trip.

From: Taste of Home

Snack Bars*
(Motor Munchies)

9 c. Rice Chex, crushed
6 c. quick-cooking oats
1 c. graham cracker crumbs
1 c. flaked coconut
1/2 c. wheat germ
2 bags (16 oz. & 10 oz.) large
  marshmallows
1 c. butter or margarine
1 1/2 c. chocolate chips, mini
  M&M's or raisins

In a very large bowl, combine the first 5 ingredients. In a saucepan, over low heat, cook and stir marshmallows and butter until the marshmallows are melted. Add honey and mix well. Pour over cereal mixture; mix well. Add chips, M&M's or raisins, if desired. Pat 2/3's into a greased 10x15x1-inch pan, and the remaining 1/3 into a 9-inch square pan. Cool. Yield: 4 to 5 dozen.

From: Taste of Home

Oatmeal Chocolate Chip Cookies*

1 c. shortening
1 c. sugar
1 c. brown sugar
2 eggs, beaten
2 c. flour
1 tsp. baking powder
2 tsp. baking soda
1 tsp. salt
2 c. quick-cooking oats
1 tsp. vanilla
1 pkg. chocolate chips
1 c. nuts, chopped

Cream sugars and shortening; add eggs and beat well after each. Add flour, baking powder, baking soda and salt; mix well. Add remaining ingredients. Mix well. Bake at 350° for about 15 minutes. Remove from oven after they have risen and fallen.
Hint: Add other goodies – raisins, coconut, etc.

Agnes Ebert

Oatmeal Macaroon Cookies*

1 c. white sugar
1 c. brown sugar
1 c. Crisco
2 eggs
1 tsp. vanilla
2 c. flour
1 tsp. baking soda
1 tsp. salt
1 tsp. baking powder
1 1/2 c. rice cereal
1 c. oatmeal (quick)

Preheat oven to 350°. Cream shortening, sugar, eggs and vanilla. Sift dry ingredients and mix well. Add cereal and oatmeal. Drop onto greased cookie sheet and press down. Bake at 350° for 8 to 10 minutes.

Thelma Hinrichs

Peanut Butter Cups*

1 roll sugar cookie dough,
　cut into 9 slices; cut each
　slice into 4ths (quarters)

Place each part into a greased miniature muffin cup. Bake 8 to 10 minutes at 350° until lightly browned. Place a miniature peanut butter cup on each cookie as it comes out of the oven. Let set for a few minutes. Remove from pan. Let cool. Yield: 36 cookies.
　Simple and tasty!

Rita Clancy

Pumpkin Patch Cookies*

4 c. flour
2 c. oatmeal
2 tsp. baking soda
2 tsp. cinnamon
1 tsp. salt
1 1/2 c. butter (1/2 shortening)
2 c. brown sugar
2 c. white sugar
1 egg
1 tsp. vanilla
16 oz. pumpkin
2 c. raisins
1 c. pecans, chopped

Mix shortening, sugars and egg. Add pumpkin and dry ingredients, nuts and raisins. Bake at 350°. Yield: 6 dozen.

Susan Martinez

Oatmeal Cookies*

2 c. margarine
2 c. brown sugar
2 c. white sugar
4 eggs
1 tsp. vanilla

Beat together.
Add:
3 c. flour
1 tsp. salt
2 tsp. baking soda
6 c. oatmeal
1 c. nuts, chopped

Drop by heaping teaspoons onto cookie sheet. Bake at 350° for about 12 minutes. Makes a large batch.
Frosting: Powdered sugar, melted butter, coffee, cinnamon and vanilla. Mix as you would for a powdered sugar frosting.
This is an old family favorite of mine, handed down for many generations.

LaVira Eggermont

Peanut Butter Cookies*

1 egg
1 c. sugar
1 c. peanut butter (plain or crunchy)

Mix ingredients – I use a mixer. Roll into balls, then roll the balls in sugar. Place on cookie sheet and flatten lightly with a fork.
If you crack the egg into the measuring cup first, your peanut butter won't stick. Do not use a dark pan – they burn easily.

Shirley Anderson

Pecan Bars*

Yellow cake mix
1 egg

1/3 c. margarine

TOPPING:
1 can sweetened condensed milk

8 oz. chocolate chips
1 egg
1 c. chopped pecans

Mix together cake mix, 1 egg and margarine. Press into greased 9x13-inch pan. Mix topping ingredients and pour over the crust. Bake 35 to 40 minutes at 350°.
When I baked for Fargo's Microsoft Corporation, this was a quick bar to prepare.

Julie Kosir Olson

Pecan Pie Bars*

2 c. unsifted flour
1/2 c. confectioners' sugar
1 c. cold margarine or butter
1 (14 oz.) can Eagle Brand sweetened condensed milk (not evaporated)

1 egg
1 tsp. vanilla extract
1 (6 oz.) pkg. almond brickle chips
1 c. chopped pecans

Preheat oven to 350° (325° for glass dish). In a medium bowl, combine flour and sugar; cut in margarine until crumbly. Press firmly onto bottom of 9x13-inch baking pan. Bake 15 minutes. Meanwhile, in a medium bowl, beat sweetened condensed milk, egg and vanilla. Stir in chips and pecans. Spread evenly over crust. Bake 25 minutes, or until golden brown. Cool; cut into bars. Yield: 36 bars.
These bars freeze very well.

Carol Miller

Perfect Frosted Creams*
(According to a 1921 cookbook)

1 c. sugar
1 c. lard
1 c. dark molasses
1 c. cold water

2 eggs
1 T. baking soda, mixed with molasses
Enough flour to make dough easy to handle

Frost with either a powder sugar frosting or a pulverized sugar frosting.

From: Ruth Society Cookbook,
Ladies Aid of Zion Methodist Church,
Tower City

Reese's Bars*

2 sticks butter or margarine
1 c. peanut butter
2 c. powdered sugar
2 c. crushed graham crackers
1 c. chocolate chips
2 T. peanut butter

Melt butter and peanut butter together in microwave. Stir in powdered sugar and graham cracker crumbs. Put in buttered 9x13-inch pan. Put in refrigerator to set. Then melt the chocolate chips and 2 tablespoons peanut butter in microwave. Spread on top of the first mixture in the pan. Yield: depends on the size that you cut the bars.

Pat Buerkle

Rice Krispie Balls*

1 (14 oz.) pkg. caramels
1 stick margarine
1/2 can Eagle Brand sweetened condensed milk

Put in a double boiler until melted. Put a large (not miniature) marshmallow on a long fork; dip in caramel, then roll in Rice Krispies. Set on waxed paper to firm up.

Ellen Moug

Rhubarb Cheesecake Bars*

CRUST:
1 c. butter
1 c. oatmeal

1 c. brown sugar
2 1/2 c. flour
Dash of salt

FILLING:
2 (8 oz.) pkg. cream cheese
1 1/2 c. sugar

3 c. rhubarb
1/2 tsp. cinnamon
1 tsp. vanilla

Crust: Mix ingredients; press 1/2 of mixture in 9x13-inch pan. Save rest for top.
Filling: Combine cream cheese with sugar, vanilla, cinnamon and rhubarb. Pour on top crust and add rest of crumbs. Bake at 350° for 40 minutes.

Susan Martinez

Rice Krispie Caramel Bars*

1/2 c. butter or margarine
1 1/2 pkg. mini marshmallows
8 c. Rice Krispies

Melt together:
1/2 c. butter
1 (14 oz.) pkg. caramels
1 can sweetened condensed milk

Divide the butter, marshmallows, Rice Krispie mix into 2 parts. Pat half into bottom of 9x15-inch greased pan.

Sprinkle other half Rice Krispies and 1/2 package marshmallows in a 9x13-inch pan, sprayed with Pam. Pour caramel mixture over. Flip the krispie layer from first pan on top and spread around with fingers.

A nice, layered, Rice Krispie bar. *Geneveive Gullickson*

Salted Nut Bars*

1 Jiffy yellow cake mix
1/2 c. butter
1 egg

Mix together and press into 9x13-inch pan. Bake 12 minutes at 350°. Add 2 1/2 cups miniature marshmallows over top of crust. Return to oven and bake 2 minutes.

While the crust is baking, melt 3/4 cup white syrup, 1/2 stick margarine or butter, 12 ounces peanut butter chips and 2 teaspoons vanilla. (I put the pan over the vent from the oven to do this.) Add 2 cups of Planters salted cocktail peanuts. Stir in 2 cups of Rice Krispies.

Put this mixture on top of the marshmallows (it is easier if you use about 1/2 cup of mixture at a time). Press down. Cut when cool. Keeps well in the refrigerator.

This is not a "quick" recipe, but it is oh so good!

Virginia Maasjo

Even if I knew certainly the world would end tomorrow,
I would plant an apple tree today.
Martin Luther

Salted Nut Roll Bars*

1 jar salted peanuts
1 (12 oz.) bag peanut butter chips
3/4 (10.5 oz.) bag mini marshmallows
3 T. butter
1 can sweetened condensed milk

Butter a 9x13-inch cake pan. Cover the bottom of the pan with salted peanuts. Melt together peanut butter chips, butter and sweetened condensed milk. Stir marshmallows in melted mixture. Pour in pan over peanuts. Put remainder of peanuts on top and press entire mix into pan with your hand. Refrigerate 1 to 2 hours. Yield: 18 to 24 bars (depending on size).

To melt mixture, use double boiler on the stove, or for even quicker method, use the microwave. **Lindsay Perlenfein**

Snicker Bars*

1 (18.25 oz.) pkg. German chocolate cake mix
3/4 c. melted butter or margarine
2/3 c. sweetened condensed milk
4 to 5 (2.16 oz.) Snickers candy bars, sliced

Preheat oven to 350°. Spray a 9x13-inch baking pan with nonstick coating. Combine cake mix, melted butter and condensed milk in a medium bowl; mix well. Spread half of the mixture into prepared baking pan. Bake at 350° for 10 minutes.

While crust is baking, cut candy bars into slices. Arrange slices on top of baked crust, cut-side down, until baked crust is completely covered. Spoon remaining batter over candy (it might be a little crumbly after setting, but that is okay).

Return to the oven and bake for an additional 20 minutes. Cool slightly before cutting. **Lynn Nichols, The Forum**

Sugar Cookie Bars*

2 tubes sugar cookie dough

Press into jellyroll pan. Top with any miniature candy bars. Bake, cut and serve. **Tammy Buhr Erickson**

Triple Chocolate Brownie Cookies*

1 (13.5 oz.) pkg. Pillsbury thick 'n fudgy walnut deluxe brownie mix
1/2 c. butter or margarine, melted
1 egg
1 c. chocolate-flavored crispy rice cereal
1 (6 oz.) pkg. (1 c.) semi-sweet chocolate chips
2/3 c. quick-cooking rolled oats

Heat oven to 350°. In a large bowl, combine brownie mix with nuts, butter and egg. Stir with spoon until well blended. Add cereal, chocolate chips and oats; mix well. Drop dough by rounded teaspoonfuls 2 inches apart onto ungreased cookie sheets. Bake at 350° for 9 to 12 minutes, or until edges are set (centers will be soft). Cool 1 minute. Remove from cookie sheets. Cool 10 minutes, or until completely cooled. Store in tightly-covered container.

Della K. Richman

Unbaked Shoestring Cookies*

1 (6 oz.) pkg. chocolate chips
1 (6 oz.) pkg. butterscotch or peanut butter chips
1 can shoestring potatoes
1 c. chopped nuts

Melt chips slowly; add potatoes and nuts. Toss until all coated. Drop by spoonfuls. Let set to cool. Best if refrigerated, to keep them firm.

Betty Kappel

Whipped Cream Krumkake*

1 c. sugar
1/2 c. butter
1/2 tsp. nutmeg
3 eggs
1/2 c. cream, whipped
2 c. flour

Beat eggs. Add sugar, whipped cream, butter and nutmeg. Add enough flour to handle easily, testing on hot iron. Place 1 teaspoon of dough on iron and bake until a very light brown. Roll quickly on stick, or press into patty shell, which can be used for ice cream or fruit.

Ann Bearfield

Yum-Yum Brownies*

2 c. flour
2 c. sugar
1/4 tsp. salt

Mix and set aside.

1 c. water
1/4 c. cocoa
1/2 c. oil
1 stick margarine
1 tsp. vanilla

Mix and boil until margarine melts. Mix with dry ingredients. Add:

2 eggs
1/2 c. buttermilk
1 tsp. baking soda

Beat together. Bake in jellyroll pan at 375° for 20 minutes.

FROSTING:
6 T. butter
6 T. milk
1 1/2 c. sugar

Bring to a boil and boil at good roll for 45 seconds. Stir in 6 ounces of semi-sweet chocolate chips. Put in cold water and stir until slightly thick.

Jane Pierce

Cooked Icing*

Beat 5 egg yolks and add 1 cup each of sugar and sour cream. Cook in a double boiler, stirring constantly until thick. Remove from heat and add 1 cup chopped black walnut meats. Spread between layers of cake, and on the top. Flavoring of your choice may be added if walnuts are not used (1 teaspoon).

From: Edith Hansen's Kitchen Show,
A long-ago radio show

The clock must be the master of the house.
Swedish proverb

Lemon Bars*

1 can sweetened condensed milk
1/2 c. lemon juice
1 tsp. grated lemon rind
1 1/2 c. flour
1 tsp. baking powder
1/2 tsp. salt
2/3 c. margarine
1 c. brown sugar, packed
1 c. quick oatmeal
1 c. chopped pecans

Blend milk, lemon juice and rind; set it aside. Cream the margarine and sugar. Add remainder of the dry ingredients and mix well, until crumbly. Pat half of the crumbly dough in a 9x13-inch ungreased pan. Spread the blended milk and lemon on top. Add the remaining half of the crumbly dough. Pat lightly. Bake at 350° for about 25 minutes.
Blue Ribbon Winner at the Beltrami County Fair.

Dana Yourd

Cake Mix Cookies*

1 box devils food cake mix
1/2 c. shortening
1 egg

Blend cake mix, shortening and egg; mix into a large ball. Shape into small balls, the size of a walnut. Place balls on greased cookie sheet, about 1-inch apart. Bake at 350° for 10 to 15 minutes. Frost.

Alma Finkes

Peanut Butter Surprise*

2/3 c. granulated sugar
1 c. honey or Karo syrup
1 c. peanut butter
1/2 box corn flakes (lg. size)

Combine first 2 ingredients; heat gently until sugar melts (do not boil). Blend in peanut butter until mixture is smooth. Stir in corn flakes and spread immediately in buttered 12x18-inch cookie sheet. Roll with rolling pin to make smooth and will also help stick together. Cut into squares or bars.

Jean Akin

White Chip-Orange Dream Cookies*

2 1/4 c. all-purpose flour
3/4 tsp. baking soda
1/2 tsp. salt
1 c. (2 sticks) butter or margarine, softened
1/2 c. granulated sugar
1/2 c. packed light brown sugar
1 egg
2 to 3 tsp. grated orange peel
2 c. (12 oz. pkg.) Nestlé Toll House Premier white morsels

Combine flour, baking soda and salt in small bowl. Beat butter, granulated sugar and brown sugar in large bowl with mixer, until creamy. Beat in egg and orange peel. Gradually beat in flour mixture. Stir in morsels. Drop dough by rounded tablespoon onto ungreased baking sheets. Bake in a preheated, 350° oven for 10 to 12 minutes, or until edges are light brown. Let stand for 2 minutes; remove to wire racks to cool completely.

From: A Nestlés ad

Notes & Recipes

Finish Line - Desserts

I made a cake and it was good.
It came out just as good cake should.
I made some tea, fragrant, strong
But, sadly, no one came along.

I made a cake and it was punk.
It rose and then it went kerplunk.
I made some tea, 'twas weak and thin,
And all that day my friends dropped in.

        Contributed by Loretta Wendlick

Finish Line – Desserts

Speed Up Baking

You can use the microwave to shorten prep time when you bake. Remove all wrappings before zapping, and use HIGH power. Soften butter or cream cheese in a microwave-safe bowl. Melt chocolate and toast nuts in a glass measure. (Spreading them on a plate will take longer; using a cup helps to concentrate the heat.) And be sure to stir chocolate and nuts twice during cooking so they heat evenly.

Softening Butter | **How long?**
6 tablespoons (3/4 stick) | 15 to 30 seconds
1/2 cup (1 stick) | 20 to 25 seconds
10 tablespoons (1 1/4 sticks) | 20 to 40 seconds
3/4 cup (1 1/2 sticks) | 30 to 45 seconds
1 cup (2 sticks) | 35 to 50 seconds

Softening cream cheese | **How long?**
3-ounce package | 15 to 20 seconds
8-ounce package | 30 seconds to 2 minutes

Melting chocolate | **How long?**
2 ounces | 45 seconds to 1 1/4 minutes
4 ounces | 1 to 2 1/4 minutes
8 ounces | 1 1/4 to 2 1/2 minutes

Melting white chocolate | **How long?**
3 ounces | 45 seconds to 1 1/2 minutes
6 ounces | 1 to 2 1/4 minutes

Toasting coconut | **How long?**
1/2 cup | 1 1/4 to 2 minutes
3/4 cup | 1 1/2 to 2 1/2 minutes
1 cup | 2 to 3 minutes

Toasting nuts | **How long?**
1/2 cup | 1 1/4 to 1 1/2 minutes
1 cup | 1 1/2 to 2 1/2 minutes

From: Good Housekeeping

Apple Dumplings

3 c. sugar
3 c. water
3/8 tsp. cinnamon
1/8 tsp. nutmeg
6 T. margarine
3 to 6 apples (depending on size), peeled & cored, cut into 1/2's, 1/4's or 1/8's

2 c. flour
1 tsp. salt
2 tsp. baking powder
3/4 c. shortening
1/2 c. milk

Mix syrup of sugar, water, cinnamon, nutmeg and butter. Bring to a boil and take off of heat. Sift flour, salt and baking powder; cut in shortening. Add milk all at once and stir until moistened. Roll dough 1/4-inch thick. Arrange the apple pieces and wrap in dough. Pat in a 9x13-inch pan and pour the syrup over the dumplings. Bake at 350° for 20 to 35 minutes.

Jennifer Fraase

Amazing Rhubarb Cobbler*

1/2 c. (1 stick) margarine
1 c. flour
2 tsp. baking powder
1/2 c. sugar
1/2 c. milk

1 c. hot water
1 c. sugar
Cinnamon
2 c. rhubarb, cut in 1/4" pieces

Melt margarine in 9-inch square pan. Make batter of flour, 1/2 cup sugar, baking powder and milk. Spoon over melted margarine. Place rhubarb over batter. Stir 1 cup sugar into the hot water until dissolved. Pour over rhubarb and sprinkle with cinnamon. Bake at 350° for 40 minutes. Serve with Cool Whip or ice cream.
Very good.

Vivian Nayes

American Berry No-Bake Cheesecake*

2 (8 oz.) pkg. Philadelphia cream cheese, softened
1/3 c. sugar
2 T. lemon juice (opt.)

1 (8 oz.) ctn. Cool Whip whipped topping, thawed, divided
1 (6 oz.) Honey Maid graham pie crust
Strawberry halves & blueberries

Beat cream cheese, sugar and lemon juice in large bowl with electric mixer on medium speed until well blended. Gently stir in 2 cups of the whipped topping. Spoon into crust. Refrigerate 3 hours, or until set. Spread Cool Whip over top. Arrange berries in rows to resemble flag.
Prep: 15 minutes plus refrigerating.

From: Cool Whip ad

Apple Crisp for One*

1 sm. cooking apple, peeled & diced
1 T. packed brown sugar
1 T. all-purpose flour
1 T. oatmeal
Dash of cinnamon (or nutmeg)
1 T. softened butter or margarine

Place apple slices in small casserole or custard cup. Mix reset of ingredients. Sprinkle over apple. Bake, uncovered, at 375° until apples are done. OR microwave on HIGH for 10 minutes, or until apples are done.

Melva Glemming

Apple Dumpling Bake*

2 (8 oz.) tubes refrigerated crescent rolls
2 med. Granny Smith apples, peeled & cored
1 c. sugar
1/3 c. butter or margarine
3/4 c. Mountain Dew soda
Ground cinnamon

Unroll crescent rolls and separate dough into 16 triangles. Cut each apple into eight wedges. Wrap a crescent dough triangle around each apple wedge. Place in a greased 9x13x2-inch baking dish. In a bowl, combine sugar and butter; sprinkle over rolls. Slowly pour the soda around the rolls (do not stir). Sprinkle with cinnamon. Bake, uncovered, at 350° for 35 to 40 minutes, or until golden brown. Serve warm with ice cream. Yield: 16 dumplings.

Marlys Freadhoff

Angel Food Dessert*

1 angel food cake mix

Put in 9x13-inch pan.

1 (20 oz.) can crushed pineapple, juice & all (not syrupy kind)
1 tsp. vanilla (added to juice)

Put pineapple on mix and stir well (in the pan). Stir, don't beat. Bake 30 to 35 minutes at 350° (might need longer, depending on oven). <u>Do not underbake – cool</u>. Cut into squares. Serve with whipped topping or pie filling.

Comes from Eagles magazine.

*Betty Kappel, Wanda Kaiser,
Melva Glemming, Bonnie Lee*

Apple Upside-Down Cake*

1 lg. Golden Delicious apple (about 1/2 lb.)
3 T. brown sugar
Vegetable cooking spray
1/4 c. sugar
1/4 c. vegetable oil
1 egg
1/2 c. dark molasses
1 1/3 c. flour
1 tsp. ground ginger
3/4 tsp. baking soda
1/2 tsp. ground cinnamon
1/4 tsp. ground cloves
1/2 c. hot water

Peel, core and slice apple crosswise into 7 rings. Combine apple rings and brown sugar in a bowl; toss gently. Let stand 5 minutes. Arrange apple mixture in a single layer in a 10-inch cast-iron skillet coated with cooking spray. Bake at 350° for 15 minutes. Combine 1/4 cup sugar, oil and egg in a large bowl. Beat 2 minutes at medium speed of an electric mixer. Add molasses; beat 2 minutes. Combine flour and next 5 ingredients. With mixer running at low speed, add to sugar mixture alternately with hot water, beginning and ending with flour mixture. Spoon batter over apple rings. Bake at 350° for 30 minutes, or until wooden pick inserted in center comes out clean. Cool in skillet 10 minutes. Invert onto serving plate.

Bonnie Lee

Black Russian Bundt Cake

1 pkg. yellow cake mix (without pudding)
1/2 c. sugar
1 (6 oz.) pkg. instant chocolate pudding
1 c. vegetable oil
4 eggs
1/4 c. vodka
1/4 c. Kahlua
3/4 c. water
Glaze (below)
Powdered sugar

Grease and flour a 12-cup bundt pan. Preheat oven to 350°. Combine cake mix, sugar, pudding mix, oil, eggs, vodka, Kahlua and water. Mix at low speed about 1 minute. Beat at medium 4 minutes. Pour into prepared pan. Bake 60 to 70 minutes. Prepare glaze. Let cake cool in pan 10 minutes; invert onto plate. Poke holes in cake with fork. Slowly pour glaze over cake. Cool completely. Sprinkle with powdered sugar. Yield: 16 to 24 servings.

Glaze: Combine 1/2 cup powdered sugar and 1/4 cup Kahlua; blend until smooth.

Audrey Gaukler

Boston Cream Pie Loaf*

1 (16 oz.) frozen poundcake, thawed
2 c. refrigerated low-fat vanilla pudding (from a 22-oz. tub)
1/2 c. double-chocolate ice cream topping

Slice poundcake into 3 layers using a long serrated knife. Place bottom layer on serving plate. Spread evenly with 1 cup pudding. Top with middle cake layer; spread with remaining pudding. Top with remaining cake layer, cut-side down. Spread with ice cream topping, pushing it gently over edges so topping drips down sides of cake. Serve immediately or refrigerate up to 3 days. Yield: 12 servings.
Preparation time: 12 minutes.

From: Woman's Day magazine

Bread Pudding for Two*

1 1/2 c. day-old buttered bread (2 slices), cubed
2 eggs
1/4 c. sugar
1/8 tsp. nutmeg
1 c. milk
1/4 tsp. cinnamon
Dash of salt

Place bread in a greased baking dish, or divide between 2 greased 8-ounce baking dishes. Set aside. In a bowl, beat eggs, milk, sugar, cinnamon, nutmeg and salt. Pour over bread. Bake, uncovered, at 350° for 40 to 45 minutes, or until a knife inserted near the center comes out clean. Cool slightly. Serve warm with a dollop of whipped cream or ice cream.

Melva Glemming

It is difficult to think anything but pleasant thoughts while eating a home-grown tomato.
Lewis Grizzard

Broiler Cake

2 eggs
1 c. sugar
1/2 c. milk
1 T. butter

1 c. flour
1 tsp. baking powder
1/8 tsp. salt
1/2 tsp. vanilla

FROSTING:
5 T. brown sugar
2 T. cream

3 T. butter
1/2 c. coconut

Beat eggs until light and add sugar gradually. Add milk and butter. Place in saucepan and bring to boiling point. Quickly fold in remaining sifted dry ingredients. Add vanilla. Turn into greased 8-inch square pan. Bake at 375° for 30 minutes.
Frosting: Combine items and boil. Spread on hot cake; place under broiler until frosting is boiling and coconut is turning brown.
Eat warm!   **Sandy Swanke DalBello via Evelyn Swanke**

Brown Stone Front Cake*

1 c. sugar
1 c. sour cream
1 c. flour
2 eggs

1 tsp. vanilla
3 T. cocoa
1 tsp. baking soda
Dash of salt

Preheat oven to 375°. Mix 1 cup sugar with sour cream; beat well. Add eggs; beat again. Add vanilla. Add flour, cocoa, baking soda and salt, sifting all together. Beat again. Pour into a 9x9-inch greased cake pan. Place on middle shelf of oven. Bake for 30 to 35 minutes (test at 30 minutes; best if not overbaked).
This was my Aunt Virginia's favorite cake – and I made it often when I worked for her. Later, it became my family's favorite (MR).
Marcella Richman via Virginia Trader

Brownie Cupcakes*

1 3/4 c. sugar
1 tsp. baking powder
4 eggs
1 tsp. vanilla
1/2 c. nuts (opt.)

1 c. flour
1 c. margarine
1 c. chocolate chips
Pinch of salt

Combine sugar, flour, baking powder and salt. Melt margarine and chocolate chips; add to flour mixture. Beat eggs slightly and add to flour mixture with vanilla. Add nuts, if desired. Fill 16 to 18 cupcake liners 2/3 full. Bake at 350° for 25 minutes.   **John Perry**

Brownie Trifle*

Brownie mix
2 sm. boxes instant chocolate
  pudding
16 oz. Cool Whip
1 or 2 lg. Symphony candy bars,
  chopped

Make brownies as directed on box. Let cool and cut into bite-size pieces. Make pudding as directed on box. In a pretty glass bowl, layer the "cut-up" brownies, then a layer of pudding, then Cool Whip, then candy bits. Repeat and chill.

This can be made the night before. All kids – young and old – love this at potlucks!

Susan McClaflin

Butterscotch Snack Cake*

1 (3 oz.) pkg. cook & serve
  butterscotch pudding mix
2 c. milk
1 yellow cake mix
1/2 c. chopped nuts
1 c. chocolate chips
1 c. butterscotch chips

In a 2-quart Pyrex mixing bowl, cook pudding in the microwave according to package directions. Stir in the yellow cake mix. Spread into a 9x13-inch cake pan sprayed with nonstick spray. Top with nuts and chips. Bake at 350° for 30 to 35 minutes. Cut while still warm.

Debbie Tuck

Caramel Dumplings

In a heavy skillet, put:
1 c. water
1/2 c. brown sugar
1 T. butter

Let come to a boil.

Drop in batter which has been mixed together:
1/2 c. cream
1 c. flour
1 tsp. baking powder
1 tsp. vanilla
Nuts, dates or coconut (opt.)

Bake in the skillet for 20 minutes at 325°. May be served hot or cold.

Margaret Schluchter,
What's Cooking, the Salem Community
and Methodist Church Cookbook, 1948

Caramel Ice Cream Sauce*

1/2 c. packed brown sugar
1 T. cornstarch
1/3 c. half & half cream
2 T. water
2 T. light corn syrup
1 T. butter or margarine
1/2 tsp. vanilla extract
Ice cream

In a saucepan, combine the brown sugar and cornstarch. Stir in the cream, water and corn syrup until smooth. Bring to a boil; cook and stir for 2 minutes, or until thickened. Remove from the heat; stir in the butter and vanilla until butter is melted. Serve warm or cold over ice cream. Refrigerate leftovers. Yield: about 1 cup.

From: Quick Cooking

Cherries and Cream Pie*

1 (3 oz.) pkg. cherry gelatin
3/4 c. boiling water
1 pt. vanilla ice cream
1 (22 oz.) can cherry pie filling
1 (10") graham crust'
Whipped dessert topping

Combine gelatin and water. Stir until dissolved. Add ice cream by spoonfuls, stirring until melted. Set aside 5 or 6 cherries from filling and blend the remaining into ice cream mixture. Pour into crumb crust and chill. To serve, top with whipped topping and reserved cherries.

Joan Dameron

Cherry-Pineapple Dessert*

1 (20 oz.) can crushed pineapple
1 can cherry pie filling

Mix and put in 9x13-inch pan.

1 white cake mix (dry)
1 cube oleo
1 c. nuts

Mix all together. Put on top of cherry-pineapple mixture. Bake at 350° for 30 to 35 minutes.

Betty Kappel

Chocolate Cake

3 c. sifted flour
2 tsp. baking soda
1 tsp. salt
1/3 c. cocoa
2 c. sugar

1 tsp. vanilla
2 T. vinegar
3/4 c. salad oil
2 c. water

Cake: Sift together into a 9x13-inch ungreased cake pan the flour, baking soda, salt, cocoa and sugar. Make 3 holes in dry ingredients and pour vanilla, vinegar and oil – one in each hole. Pour water over the batter and blend with a fork until smooth. Bake in a moderate oven (350°) for 30 to 40 minutes.

Frosting: In a saucepan, add 1 1/2 cups sugar (less is okay), 5 tablespoons milk and 5 tablespoons butter. Bring to a rolling boil (can use margarine, but don't short milk). Immediately pour into blender. Add 1 cup semi-sweet chocolate chips. Blend mixture until smooth and work quickly to spread it on the cake before mixture sets.

Blue ribbon winner at the Beltrami County Fair.

Dana Yourd

Chocolate Cake

1 tsp. baking soda
2 sq. baking chocolate

1/2 c. boiling water

Stir and let stand while next part is mixed.

1 1/2 c. sugar

1/2 c. butter

Cream together.

Add:
2 eggs, beaten
1/2 c. buttermilk or sour cream

1 tsp. vanilla
2 c. flour

Add baking soda, chocolate and water; beat well. Pour into 9x12-inch greased cake pan. Bake 30 to 40 minutes at 350°.

Bernita Landgrebe Voelker,
From: St. Paul's Cookbook, 1950

Chocolate Vinegar Cake

3 c. flour
1/2 c. dry cocoa
2 c. sugar
2 tsp. baking soda
1 tsp. salt

1 c. salad oil
2 c. water
2 T. vinegar
2 tsp. vanilla

Mix all ingredients together with mixer. Pour into greased and floured 9x13-inch pan. Bake 30 to 35 minutes at 350°. Cool. Frost with fudge frosting (recipe below).

FUDGE FROSTING:
1/2 c. butter or margarine

1 c. sugar
4 T. milk

Bring to full boil. Boil 2 minutes. Remove from heat and add:
1 c. mini marshmallows   1 c. chocolate chips

Beat until chips and marshmallows are melted and frosting is spreading consistency.
This is the only chocolate cake our family makes. So easy the grandchildren make it.

Liz Outram

Cool and Creamy Coconut Cake

This cake is best prepared a day or two ahead so all the liquid gets absorbed.

1 (18.25 oz.) box yellow cake mix
1 (14 oz.) can sweetened
   condensed milk
1 (12 oz.) can cream of coconut

1 (8 oz.) ctn. frozen whipped topping, thawed
2 1/2 to 3 c. flaked, sweetened coconut

Heat oven to 350°. Grease a 9x13x2-inch baking pan. Prepare cake mix as package directs. Pour batter into pan; bake as box directs. Remove from oven and, using a fork or skewer, poke holes in entire cake. Mix condensed milk and cream of coconut; slowly pour over warm cake. Cool cake completely. Frost with topping; sprinkle with coconut. Cover and refrigerate until serving. Cut in squares.
A fabulous light cake!

Ann Cease

Chocolate Chip Cookie Mousse*

1 roll refrigerated chocolate chip cookie dough
1 (8 oz.) pkg. cream cheese
1/3 c. sugar
1 (3.9 oz.) pkg. <u>instant</u> chocolate pudding (chocolate fudge)
1 pt. liquid whipping cream
Optional toppings: grated chocolate or vanilla chips, whipped cream/Cool Whip, nuts

Slice dough in approximately 1/2-inch slices and place on baking stone or nonstick cooking sheets. Spread across stone, forming a crust (if dough is sticky, wet hands with cold water). Bake at 350° to 375° for approximately 15 minutes, until cookie is evenly browned to make a crust. Let cool 5 minutes. Slide spatula under crust to loosen. Finish cooling. Mix cream cheese with sugar. Spread on cooled crust. Mix pudding with whipping cream until set, about 5 minutes. Spread over cream cheese layer. Garnish with whipped cream flowerettes and chocolate shavings or shaved white chocolate and nuts.

From: Pampered Chef

Chocolate Pie
(Nuisance-Free)

1/2 lb. (32) lg. marshmallows
1/4 c. milk
1/8 tsp. salt
2 env. (2 oz.) no-melt unsweetened chocolate
1 tsp. vanilla
1 c. heavy cream, whipped
1 baked 8" pastry shell

Combine marshmallows, milk and salt in saucepan. Cook over moderate heat, stirring constantly, until marshmallows melt. Remove from heat. Add no-melt unsweetened chocolate and vanilla. Stir until blended. Cool thoroughly. Fold in whipped cream. Spoon into baked pie shell. Chill until set (several hours or overnight), or freeze and wrap securely and store in freezer. Yield: 1 (8-inch) pie.

My grandchildren's favorite.

Elsie (Haskins) Smaciarz

Cranberry Crisp

4 c. whole berry cranberry sauce
   (2 1-pound cans)
2 ripe pears, peeled & cut into
   1 1/2" chunks
1 tsp. grated lime zest
1/4 c. fresh lime juice
1 tsp. ground cinnamon
1/2 tsp. ground cardamom
1/4 c. all-purpose flour
1/4 c. firmly-packed brown sugar
3/4 c. oatmeal or graham cracker
   crumbs
6 T. cold, unsalted butter, cut in
   thick slices

Preheat oven to 375°. Spray an 8x8-inch glass or metal baking dish. In a bowl, stir together cranberry sauce, pears, lime zest, lime juice, cinnamon and cardamom. Pour into the prepared baking dish. In a medium bowl, stir together the flour, brown sugar and oats until well blended. Using a pastry blender or your fingers, cut the butter into the flour until it resembles a kind of meal. Scatter this mixture over the cranberry mixture. Dabble a little water over the top. Bake for 45 minutes, or until top is crisp and berries are bubbling. Serve warm or chilled. Yield: 6 servings.
   Wonderful with vanilla ice cream.

Amanda Richman

Creamy Lemon Pie

1/2 c. lemon juice
1 can sweetened condensed milk
2 egg yolks
1 prepared pie crust in pie pan*

*Bake 10 minutes at 325° to 350° (if you want browner crust).
   Mix lemon juice and sweetened condensed milk. Beat egg yolks. Add to first 2 ingredients. Pour into 8-inch pie crust. Bake 30 minutes at 325° until set. Cool and serve, topped with whipped cream or Cool Whip. Drizzle raspberry syrup over for dash of color and interesting taste appeal.

Curt Brown,
From: Another Time – House of Good Food

Daddy's Rice Pudding

3 c. cooked rice
2 c. milk
1/2 c. sugar
1/4 c. butter
2 cinnamon sticks
1 tsp. vanilla extract
Ground cinnamon & sugar

Combine rice, milk, sugar, butter and cinnamon sticks in 2-quart saucepan. Stirring often, cook over medium heat for about 20 minutes until thick and creamy. Remove cinnamon sticks; stir in vanilla. Sprinkle with cinnamon sugar. Serve warm. Yield: 6 servings.

Lyn Nichols,
The Forum

Decadent Triple Layer Mud Pie*

3 sq. Baker's semi-sweet baking chocolate, melted
1/4 c. canned sweetened condensed milk
1 (6 oz.) Oreo pie crust
1/2 c. chopped toasted Planter's pecans (opt.)
2 c. cold milk
2 (4-serving size) pkg. Jello chocolate flavor instant pudding & pie filling
1 (8 oz.) ctn. Cool Whip whipped topping, thawed

Mix chocolate and condensed milk until well blended. Pour into crust; sprinkle with pecans. Pour milk into large bowl. Add pudding mixes. Beat with wire whisk 2 minutes, or until well blended (mixture will be thick). Spoon 1 1/2 cups of the pudding over pecans in crust. Add 1/2 of the whipped topping to remaining pudding; stir with wire whisk until well blended. Spread over pudding in crust; top with remaining whipped topping. Refrigerate 3 hours. Yield: 10 servings.
Preparation time: 15 minutes plus refrigerating.

From: Jello, Baker's Chocolate ad

Daiquiri Dessert*

1/2 tube Ritz crackers, crushed
1/2 c. powdered sugar
1/2 c. melted butter

Mix together and pat into bottom of 9x13-inch cake pan, reserving about 1/4 cup to sprinkle on top.

FILLING:
1 (12 oz.) ctn. Cool Whip
1 can sweetened condensed milk
1 (10 oz.) can frozen daiquiri mix

Mix these 3 ingredients together, then pour over the crust, topping with the reserved crumbs. Freeze.

Janice Diemert via Marlys Miller

Easy Dessert

1 pkg. white cake mix
1 c. chopped rhubarb
Brown sugar
Nuts

Prepare cake mix according to package directions; stir in rhubarb. Pour into greased 9x13-inch cake pan. Sprinkle a mixture of brown sugar and nuts on top. Bake as directed. Serve with ice cream.

Mrs. J.S.

Easy Lemon Dessert

1 box lemon cake mix
1/2 c. butter
1 c. sugar
1/4 c. water
1 egg, well beaten
3 T. lemon juice
Grated rind of 1 lemon
8 oz. whipped topping (Cool Whip)

Bake cake mix as directed on box, in a 9x13-inch pan. Cool. Place all other ingredients, except topping, in a saucepan and cook over medium heat, stirring constantly, just until mixture comes to a boil. Makes 1 1/3 cups. Top each piece of cake with a dollop of Cool Whip and 1 to 2 tablespoons of lukewarm lemon sauce. Sauce will keep several days in refrigerator. Yield: 12 generous servings.

Leone Osmon

Easy Rice Pudding

1 (3 oz.) pkg. vanilla pudding pie filling, <u>not instant</u>
1/2 can seedless raisins
1/2 c. quick-cooking rice
2 1/2 c. milk

Combine all ingredients in a deep 1-quart microwaveable casserole. Heat, uncovered, in the microwave oven for 6 to 8 minutes, or until mixture boils. Stir occasionally during the last 3 to 4 minutes. Serve either hot or chilled. May sprinkle with cinnamon to accent.

Marcella Richman

No one who cooks, cooks alone. Even at her most solitary, a cook in the kitchen is surrounded by generations of cooks past, the advice and menus of cooks present, the wisdom of cookbook writers.
Laurie Colwin

Fast Frostings

NUMBER 1:
2 T. creamy peanut butter   1 can white frosting

Mix together. Add 2 more tablespoons, if you want a darker, more flavorful frosting.

Clara Mayer

NUMBER 2:
1 can white frosting   1/2 c. chopped or ground walnuts
1/2 c. ground raisins   1/4 c. toasted coconut

Mix all together. Very good on plain whit e cake, cupcakes or as angel food topping. If frosting needs to be thinned for ease in spreading, add a tablespoon milk or cream. May also add extra vanilla (1 teaspoon)

Florence Cease

SOUR CREAM FILLING: Not so fast!
1/2 c. sugar   1 tsp. vanilla
1 c. sour cream   1/2 c. walnuts, chopped
3 egg yolks

Cook and stir over medium heat until mixture thickens.

*From: Ruth Society Cookbook,
Ladies Aid of Zion Methodist Church, Tower City, ND, 1921*

Fast Frosty Dessert Pie

1 pt. cream, whipped   1 c. chopped walnuts
1/2 box coconut macaroons,   3 T. sugar
  crushed   1 qt. sherbet, any flavor

Combine whipped cream, sugar, nuts, and all but a few of the crumbs. Put a layer of cream mixture in 9-inch Pie Taker Tray. Freeze. Then spread a layer of the softened sherbet on top of the frozen cream. Spread balance of cream mixture and garnish with crumbs. Freeze. Serve.

Ann Cease

Fluffy Frozen Peanut Butter Pie*

1 (8 oz.) pkg. cream cheese
1 1/2 c. powdered sugar
1 c. peanut butter
1 c. milk
1 (8 oz.) ctn. Cool Whip
2 (9") graham cracker pie shells
1/2 c. chopped peanuts

Whip cheese at low speed until soft and fluffy. Beat in sugar and peanut butter at medium speed. Slowly beat in milk. Fold in topping (Cool Whip). Pour in the pie shells. Sprinkle each pie with 1/4 cup chopped peanuts. Freeze until firm.

Susan Martinez

Fresh Peach Pie*

4 fresh peaches, peeled
20 lg. marshmallows
1/4 c. milk
1 c. whipped cream, sweetened, or Cool Whip

CRUST:
11 whole graham crackers
   (about 1 1/3 c. crumbs)
5 T. unsalted butter
1/2 c. old-fashioned oatmeal
3 T. packed brown sugar
1 tsp. vanilla extract
1/8 tsp. salt

Filling: Melt marshmallows and milk. Cool. Add sliced peaches. Add whipped cream.
Crust: Preheat oven to 350°. Place graham crackers and oatmeal in food processor and process until finely-ground. Stir in brown sugar. Add melted butter and vanilla. Stir until mixture is moistened. Press mixture evenly into 9-inch pie plate. Bake 6 minutes. Let cool.
Pour filling into cooled crust. Refrigerate. Yield: 1 (9-inch) crust.
Note: The crust may be made ahead, wrapped in plastic and frozen up to 1 month. Quick and simple pie dessert.

Clarice Dancer

Frozen Berry Fluff*

2 (21 oz.) cans raspberry pie
   filling
14 oz. sweetened condensed milk
8 oz. crushed pineapple in juice
12 oz. Cool Whip, or other whipped
   topping

Combine pie filling, milk and pineapple. Fold in Cool Whip. Pour into 9x13-inch pan. Cover and freeze 8 hours or overnight. Remove 15 minutes or longer before serving.
Note: Can split into multiple containers.

Lyndi Dittmer-Perry

Fruit Casserole*

2 cans cherry pie filling
1/2 c. tsp. cinnamon
1 lg. can pears, drained
1 lg. can mandarin oranges, drained
1 lg. can apricots, drained
1 lg. can pineapple chunks, drained
1 lg. can peaches, drained

Mix together in large covered casserole dish. Bake at 300°, covered, for 1 hour.
Hint: Good served cold also.

Rosamond Swanke Testa

Hot Fudge Sauce

1 can Carnation evaporated milk
4 sq. unsweetened chocolate
1 tsp. vanilla
2 c. sugar
1/4 lb. butter
1/2 tsp. salt (opt.)

Blend evaporated milk and sugar in a heavy 2-quart saucepan over medium heat, stirring constantly. Heat to boiling and then moderate temperature as needed to maintain boiling without boiling over. Continue to stir while boiling for at least 1 more minute. Add chocolate squares and continue to stir, but do not bring back to boiling. Stir in chocolate until smooth. Remove from heat and allow to cool for 10 minutes. Add butter, vanilla and salt, stirring to melt and blend ingredients. Yield: 2 cups.
Keeps well in refrigerator. Texture improves with every reheating.

Ellen-Earle Chaffee

Hot Fudge Sauce*

1 c. white sugar
3 tsp. cocoa
1 tsp. vanilla flavoring
1/3 c. milk
1/2 stick margarine

Combine ingredients in saucepan and slowly cook on stove until margarine is melted and all mixed together. Serve over ice cream.

Christine C. Worthen

Hurry-Up Luscious Angel Food Cake Topping*

1 (12 oz.) ctn. Cool Whip
1 c. Mrs. Richardson's caramel topping, room temp.

In a large bowl, fold the caramel topping into the Cool Whip. <u>Do not beat</u>! Cut the angel food cake into 3 layers across. Frost layers and replace, then frost the outside of cake. Refrigerate until ready to serve.

Sharon Smith

Ice Cream

7 c. milk
8 eggs, beaten
3 c. sugar
2 T. flour or cornstarch
1/8 tsp. salt
4 tsp. vanilla
6 c. cream

Heat milk; add beaten eggs, sugar, salt and flour (add slowly). Cook until a little thick. Beat with mixer. Cool. Add vanilla and cream. Put in ice cream freezer. Yield: 5 quarts.

Leona Schumacher Schock

Ice Cream Pie

1/4 c. Karo syrup
2 T. brown sugar
3 T. butter or margarine

Bring to a boil and remove from heat. Add 2 1/2 cups Rice Krispies. Mix well and press into buttered pie pan.
Mix:
1/3 c. peanut butter
1/3 c. fudge sauce
3 T. Karo syrup

Put 2/3 of mix on Rice Krispies and freeze until firm. Place ice cream (about 1 quart) on top of mixture. Drizzle remainder of mix on top. Freeze.

Esther Haa

Irish Bread Pudding with Caramel Sauce

1/4 c. light butter, melted	1 T. vanilla extract
1 (10 oz.) French bread baguette, cut into 1" thick slices	1 (12 oz.) can evaporated fat-free milk
	2 lg. eggs, lightly beaten
1/2 c. raisins	Cooking spray
1/4 c. Irish whiskey	1 T. sugar
1 3/4 c. 1% low-fat milk	1 tsp. ground cinnamon
1 c. sugar	Caramel Sauce

Preheat oven to 350°. Brush melted butter on one side of French bread slices and place bread, buttered-sides up, on a baking sheet. Bake bread at 350° for 10 minutes, or until lightly toasted. Cut bread into 1/2-inch cubes. Combine raisins and whiskey in a small bowl; cover and let stand 10 minutes, or until soft (do not drain). Combine 1% low-fat milk and next 4 ingredients in a large bowl; stir well with a whisk. Add bread cubes and raisin mixture, pressing gently to moisten; let stand 15 minutes. Spoon bread mixture into a 9x13-inch baking dish coated with cooking spray. Combine 1 tablespoon sugar and cinnamon; sprinkle over pudding. Bake at 350° for 35 minutes, or until set. Serve warm with Caramel Sauce. Yield: 12 servings, serving size 1 (3-inch) square and 2 tablespoons sauce.

I never ate bread pudding until this – it's good.

Doris Sauerland,
From: Cooking Lite

Good-To-Go Graham-Apple Stack-Ups*

When you need a quick dessert and there is no time to run to the store.

Put one graham cracker on as many plates as you need for serving. Then top each cracker with a heaping tablespoon of applesauce. Next, put a tablespoon of whipped topping over applesauce. Repeat, stacking another cracker on first layer, then applesauce, then topping. End with a graham cracker and topping. Garnish with a maraschino cherry.

This works best if it sits for awhile before serving – so make it before you have the main course.

Marcella Richman via Irma Swanke

Grandma's Autumn Apple Cake

3 eggs
1 3/4 c. sugar
1 c. oil
2 c. flour
1 tsp. cinnamon
1 tsp. baking soda
1 tsp. salt
1 tsp. vanilla
2 c. sliced apples, peeled & cored
1 c. walnuts

Beat eggs and sugar together. Add oil a little at a time. Then add salt, flour and dry ingredients to mixture. Add vanilla; fold in apples and nuts. Pour batter into greased and floured bundt pan. Bake at 350° for 40 to 50 minutes. Once pan has cooled, transfer cake to decorative dish and sprinkle powdered sugar on top. Enjoy!
 This cake is incredible, moist and excellent served while warm with a tall glass of milk or hot tea.
 I like to mix this recipe all together in my kitchen aid.

From the internet/AOL

Granny's Peach Cobbler*

1 (29 oz.) can sliced peaches, with syrup
1 (18 oz.) pkg. yellow cake mix
1/2 c. melted butter or margarine

Spread peaches in a greased 9x13-inch pan. Sprinkle dry cake mix over all. Drizzle margarine over cake mix. Bake at 325° for 45 to 55 minutes. Yield: 8 servings.

Rita Clancy

Kids Quick Ice Cream*

SUPPLIES:
Sandwich-size Ziploc bag
Gallon-size Ziploc bag

1/3 c. milk
1 T. sugar
1/8 tsp. vanilla
Ice cubes
Salt

In small bag, combine sugar, milk and vanilla. Zip shut. Drop small bag into large bag with ice cubes and 1 tablespoon salt. Shake bag with a partner until ice cream consistency forms.
 A fun science lesson, and the ice cream tastes great!

Claudia Richman Nelson

Lemon Bundt Cake

1 (18 1/4 oz.) pkg. lemon cake mix
1 (3.4 oz.) pkg. instant lemon
   pudding mix
4 eggs
1 c. water
1/3 c. vegetable oil
1 T. butter or margarine, melted
1/4 c. orange juice
1 c. confectioners' sugar

In a mixing bowl, combine dry cake and pudding mixes, eggs, water and oil. Beat on medium speed for 2 minutes. Pour into a greased and floured 10-inch fluted tube pan. Bake at 350° for 35 to 40 minutes, or until a toothpick inserted near the center comes out clean. Cool on a wire rack for 6 to 8 minutes.

Meanwhile, for glaze, combine butter and orange juice in a small bowl; stir in confectioners' sugar until smooth. Remove cake from pan to a serving platter; poke holes in cake with a meat fork. Slowly drizzle with glaze. Cool completely. Yield: 10 to 12 servings.

Convenient lemon cake and lemon pudding mixes hurry along this moist glazed cake.

From: Quick Cooking magazine

Lemon Cheesecake Dessert

1 1/2 c. graham cracker crumbs
   (about 24 sq.)
1/3 c. finely-chopped pecans
1/3 c. sugar
1/3 c. butter or margarine, melted
2 (8 oz.) pkg. cream cheese, softened
1 (14 oz.) can sweetened condensed
   milk
2 eggs
1/2 c. lemon juice

In a bowl, combine the cracker crumbs, pecans and sugar. Add butter; mix well. Set aside 1/2 cup. Press the remaining crumb mixture into a greased 9x13x2-inch baking dish. Bake at 325° for 8 minutes.

Meanwhile, in a small mixing bowl, beat the cream cheese until smooth. Add the milk, eggs and lemon juice; beat until smooth. Spoon over crust. Sprinkle with the reserved crumb mixture. Bake for 30 minutes, or until center is almost set. Cool on a wire rack. Store in the refrigerator. Yield: 16 to 20 servings.

Peggy Key,
From: Quick Cooking magazine,

Lemon Cream Dessert

1 1/2 c. sugar
1/3 c. + 1 T. cornstarch
1 1/2 c. cold water
3 egg yolks, lightly beaten
3 T. butter or margarine, softened
2 tsp. grated lemon peel
1/2 c. lemon juice
1 c. all-purpose flour
1 c. finely-chopped walnuts
1/2 c. butter or margarine, softened
1 (8 oz.) pkg. cream cheese, softened
1 c. confectioners' sugar
2 c. cold milk
2 (3.4 oz.) pkg. instant vanilla pudding
1 tsp. vanilla
1 (16 oz.) ctn. Cool Whip, thawed

Second topping (ingredients 1 to 7): In a small saucepan, combine sugar and cornstarch. Gradually stir in water until smooth. Bring to boil. Cook and stir 1 minute. Remove from heat. Stir in small amount of hot filling into egg yolks. Stir this back into saucepan. Return to heat. Bring to boil. Boil and stir 1 minute. Remove from heat; add butter and lemon peel. Gently stir in lemon juice. Refrigerate until cool.

Crust (double if you like a thicker crust): In a bowl combine next 3 ingredients (flour, walnuts and margarine). Cut butter into flour and walnuts until crumbly. Press into greased 9x13-inch pan. Bake at 350° for 15 to 20 minutes.

First Topping: In mixing bowl, beat cream cheese and sugar until smooth. Spread over cooled crust. Spread cooled lemon mixture over cream cheese topping,

Third and Fourth Toppings (last 4 ingredients): In another mixing bowl, beat milk and pudding mixes on low for 2 minutes. Beat in vanilla. Fold in 1/2 of Cool Whip. Pour over lemon layer. Spread remaining Cool Whip over top.

Chill at least 4 hours or overnight. Yield: 18 to 24 servings.

Mary Buringrud

It seems to me that our three basic needs, for food and security and love, are so entwined that we cannot think of one without the other.
M. F. K. Fisher

Lemon Crumb Pie

CRUMB CRUST:
About 12 single-square graham crackers (to yield 1 1/2 c. crumbs)
1/4 c. sugar
5 to 6 T. butter, melted

LEMON FILLING:
3 lg. eggs
2 lemons
1 (14 oz.) can sweetened condensed milk
1/8 tsp. salt

Crust: Spread the crackers in a single layer on a piece of waxed paper. Cover with another piece of waxed paper. Roll a rolling pin over the crackers, pressing down as you roll, so the crackers are reduced to fine crumbs. Measure the crumbs. You'll need 1 1/2 cups. Combine the sugar and crumbs; stir to blend evenly. Pour the melted butter into the crumb mixture. Use your hands to stir and toss until the butter is well-mixed into the crumbs. Set aside 1/4 cup of the crumb mixture to sprinkle on top of the pie. Press the larger amount of crumb mixture into the bottom and up the sides of a 9-inch pie pan. Cover and refrigerate while you mix the filling.

Filling: Preheat the oven to 325°. Separate the egg yolks from the whites. Put the yolks into a mixing bowl and stir briskly with a fork until well blended. Grate the zest of the lemons, then finely chop. Add to the yolks. Cut the lemons in half and juice them. Strain the juice; discard the seeds. Add the lemon juice to the yolks and beat until thoroughly blended. Stir in the condensed milk and salt. Blend thoroughly. Beat the egg whites until they are stiff enough to hold a peak on the end of the beater. Fold the whites into the yolk mixture until the mixture is all one color.

Spoon the filling into the crumb-lined pan. Sprinkle the reserved crumbs evenly over the top. Bake for about 40 minutes. Yield: 8 servings.

This is good served slightly warm, at room temperature or cold.

From: Arizona Daily Star

Soul food is just what the name implies. It is soulfully cooked food or richly flavored food, good for your ever-loving soul.
Sheila Ferguson

Mama's Applesauce Cake
(From The Waltons)

1/2 c. butter, softened	2 c. raisins
1 c. packed light brown sugar	1 c. granulated sugar
1 T. + 1 tsp. baking soda	3 c. applesauce
1 tsp. salt	2 tsp. cinnamon
1 tsp. cloves	1 tsp. nutmeg
1/2 c., or more, chopped pecans or walnuts	2 3/4 c. all-purpose flour

Cream shortening and sugars. Combine applesauce and baking soda; add to creamed mixture, beating until blended. Add flour, salt and spices; mix until smooth. Stir in nuts and raisins. Spoon into greased 9x13-inch cake pan and bake at 350° for 45 minutes, or until cake tests done. Or bake in a tube pan at 350° for 1 hour, or until cake tests done.

Nancy Houge,
Judy Wray

Mandarin Cake*

1 yellow cake mix	1 (11 oz.) can mandarin oranges, with juice
3 eggs	
3/4 c. oil	

Bake in 9x13-inch pan as directed on cake box.

TOPPING:
8 oz. Cool Whip
1 pkg. instant vanilla pudding
1 (20 oz.) can crushed pineapple

Take juice from pineapple to mix pudding. Then add to the rest.
Cake is very moist. The topping keeps for days. I use topping on the cake as I serve it. The cake freezes well.

Ann Loh

Microwave Apple Crisp*

6 c. sliced, peeled apples	1/2 c. flour
1/4 c. butter	3/4 c. packed brown sugar
1/2 c. quick-cooking oats	1 tsp. cinnamon

Spread apple slices in 8x8-inch baking dish. Cut butter into mixture of oats, flour, brown sugar and cinnamon in bowl until crumbly. Sprinkle over apples. Microwave on HIGH for 12 to 15 minutes, or until apples are tender. Serve warm or cold with whipped cream or ice cream. May substitute fresh peaches for apples.

Carol Thompson

Microwave Cherry Crisp*

1 can cherry pie filling (or blueberry, peach or your favorite)
3/4 c. brown sugar
2/3 c. oatmeal
1/3 c. flour
1/4 c. butter

Grease (or spray) 1 microwave pie pan. Pour in pie filling. Combine sugar, oatmeal and flour. Cut in butter, as if for pie crust. Sprinkle crumb mixture over fruit filling. Microwave on HIGH for 12 to 14 minutes, or until mixture bubbles. Let cool for 20 minutes or so, before serving.

Mae Triebold

Mini Cheesecakes*

12 vanilla wafer cookies
16 oz. cream cheese, softened
1/2 c. sugar
1 tsp. vanilla
2 eggs

Line 12 muffin tins with foil liners. Place 1 vanilla wafer in each liner. Mix cream cheese, vanilla and sugar on medium heat until well blended. Add eggs. Mix well. Pour mixture over wafers, filling 3/4 full. Bake at 325° for 25 minutes. Remove from pan when cool. Chill. Top with fruit, preserves, nuts or chocolate.

John Perry

Mini Upside-Down Pineapple Cakes

2 (20 oz.) cans pineapple slices
1/3 c. margarine, melted
2/3 c. packed brown sugar
1 (18.25 oz.) pkg. yellow cake mix
Red raspberries or maraschino cherries
Slivered almonds (opt.)

Drain pineapple and reserve juice. In a bowl, stir together melted margarine and brown sugar. Evenly divide sugar mixture into 3-inch greased muffin cups. Arrange pineapple over sugar mixture. Prepare cake mix according to package directions, replacing water with reserved juice. Pour batter into prepared muffin cups. Bake in a 350° oven for 20 to 25 minutes, or until toothpick inserted in center comes out clean. Cool for 5 minutes. Loosen edges with a knife and invert onto serving platter. Place raspberries or cherries in center of pineapple slices and sprinkle with a few slivered almonds. Yield: 20 servings.

Lyn Nichols,
The Forum

Missionary Cake*

1 c. flour
1 c. sugar
1 tsp. baking soda
1/2 tsp. salt
1 (No. 2) can fruit cocktail, drained
1 egg
1/2 c. brown sugar
1/2 c. nuts, chopped

Sift all dry ingredients, except brown sugar and nuts. Add well-drained fruit cocktail and egg. Beat well until rather thin. Pour into 9x9-inch greased pan. Sprinkle brown sugar and nuts on top. Bake at 350° for 40 minutes.
Hint: Double recipe for 9x13-inch pan.

Agnes Swanke Ebert

My Mom's Hot Fudge Sauce*

1 c. sugar (white or half white/ half brown)
1/2 c. evaporated milk
1/4 c. butter
2 oz. unsweetened baking chocolate, chopped up
Pinch of salt

Combine everything in a saucepan and stir over medium heat until it boils. Boil 1 minute. Serve over ice cream.

Lori Powell Gordon,
"If my house was on fire...these are the recipes I'd take" Cookbook

No-Bake Lemon Cheesecake

2 (3 oz.) pkg. lemon gelatin
2 c. boiling water
1 c. cold water
8 oz. light cream cheese
1 c. nonfat sour cream
1/4 c. sugar
1 tsp. vanilla extract
1/2 c. orange marmalade

Dissolve gelatin in boiling water in large bowl. Stir in cold water. Chill for 1 hour, or until partially set. Combine cream cheese with sour cream, sugar and vanilla in mixer bowl; beat until smooth. Add to gelatin; beat for 5 minutes, or until smooth. Spoon into 9-inch springform pan. Chill for 4 hours, or until set. Loosen edge with spatula dipped into hot water. Place on serving plate; remove side of pan. Spread marmalade gently over top. Chill until serving time. Yield: 12 servings.
Variation: May substitute apricot jam for orange marmalade.

Cindy Heidt

Oatmeal Cake

1 1/2 c. boiling water
1 c. quick oatmeal
1/2 c. butter
1 c. brown sugar
1 c. white sugar
2 eggs
1 1/2 c. flour
1/2 tsp. salt
1 tsp. vanilla

Pour boiling water over oats and let stand 20 minutes. Cream butter and sugars. Add eggs. Add other ingredients. Add soaked oatmeal. Bake in a 9x13-inch pan, which has been sprayed with cooking oil. Bake for 35 minutes at 350°.

FROSTING:
1/2 c. butter
1 c. brown sugar
1/2 c. whipping cream (not whipped)

Boil gently for 10 minutes, stirring often.
Add:
1 tsp. vanilla
1 c. coconut
1/2 c. chopped nuts

Mix together and let stand until cool. Beat and frost the cake.

Pat Buerkle

Orange Cake

Orange cake mix
1 pkg. orange Jello
2 eggs
1/2 c. oil
1 1/2 c. water

Mix all the ingredients and bake as directed on the cake mix box, in a 9x13-inch pan at 350° for 1 hour.

FROSTING:
4 oz. cream cheese
1 (8 oz.) can crushed pineapple
1 (8 oz.) ctn. Cool Whip
1 pkg. instant vanilla pudding
1 T. sugar
3/4 c. orange juice

Mix all ingredients.
Note: I don't frost cake until shortly before I'm ready to serve it.
This cake makes a nice "springtime" cake. It is a good cake to serve at Easter. Also, the only place I have found the orange cake mix is at Marketplace in Valley City.

Beth Pedersen

Orange Cake

1 1/2 c. brown sugar
1/2 c. shortening
2 eggs
1/2 c. sour milk
1 tsp. baking soda
1 c. raisins, ground
1 orange, grind, peel & all
2 c. flour

Cream shortening and sugar. Add well-beaten eggs. Dissolve baking soda in sour milk and add alternately with the sifted flour. Add ground orange and raisins. Nuts may be added also. Bake in a greased 8- or 9-inch square pan, or large loaf pan, at 325° for 40 minutes, or until tests done.
Delicious for brunch/lunch.

Agnes Schneekloth,
From: St. Paul's Lutheran Ladies Aid, 1950

Pineapple Dessert

16 oz. marshmallows
2 c. milk

Melt together and add 1 1/2 teaspoons lemon extract. Drain 1 can crushed pineapple. Add to cooled marshmallow mixture. Whip 1 pint cream, adding 1 tablespoon powdered sugar. Fold into the pineapple mixture. Fold into a graham cracker crust made of 32 crushed graham crackers, 1/2 stick of butter and 1 teaspoon sugar. Put in bottom of a 9x13-inch cake pan, reserving about 1/4 cup for topping. (Or you can use 2 prepared crumb pie crusts if you are in a hurry, using a topping of your choice.)

Juanita Beilke

Pineapple Dessert

CRUST:
18 graham crackers, crushed
1/2 c. butter, melted
3 T. powdered sugar

FILLING:
1 pkg. marshmallows
1/2 c. milk
2 c. cream
1 (20 oz.) can crushed pineapple

Crust: Mix together and put in 9x13-inch pan. Save 1/2 for top. Put in 350° oven for 5 minutes.
Filling: Put marshmallows and milk in double boiler until melted. Whip cream and fold in marshmallow mixture and pineapple. Top with crumbs. Chill in freezer drawer of refrigerator.

Susan Martinez

Pineapple Snow*

1 c. crushed pineapple or
   pineapple tidbits, drained
   (reserve juice)
1 c. mini marshmallows
1/2 c. quartered maraschino cherries
1 c. Cool Whip
2 to 3 T. pineapple juice
1/2 c. slivered almonds

Mix together. Refrigerate in a bowl, or transfer to a crumb pie shell (Oreo crust or graham cracker).
Makes a light, tasty dessert or salad.

From: Radio Talk Show

Peppermint Ice Cream Cake

This is the kind of dessert that's perfect for any special occasion. What's also nice is the fact that the cake can be made a few days ahead and stored in the freezer until the celebration starts.

4 c. crisp rice cereal
1 (7 oz.) milk chocolate candy bar
1/2 c. butter or margarine
1/2 gal. peppermint stick ice cream, softened
2 c. whipped topping
Peppermint candy canes or crushed peppermint candies

Place cereal in a large bowl. Grate or shave 2 tablespoons of chocolate from candy bar; set aside. In a heavy saucepan, melt butter and remaining chocolate. Pour over cereal and stir to coat. Press into the bottom of a greased 10-inch springform pan. Freeze for 30 minutes. Spoon ice cream over crust. Freeze for 15 minutes. Spread with whipped topping; sprinkle wit h the shaved chocolate. Cover and freeze for several hours or overnight. Top with candy. Remove cake from freezer 5 to 10 minutes before serving. Remove sides of pan; cut with a sharp knife and serve immediately. Yield: 8 to 10 servings.

From: A Magazine insert

The table is a meeting place, a gathering ground, the source of sustenance and nourishment, festivity, safety and satisfaction.
Laurie Colwin

Pumpkin Pie Cake

CRUST:
Yellow cake mix (save 1 c. for topping)
1/2 c. softened margarine
1 egg

Mix and press into a greased 9x13-inch pan.

FILLING:
1 can pumpkin
3 eggs
2 tsp. cinnamon
1 c. sugar
2/3 c. evaporated milk

Mix and pour over crust.

TOPPING:
1 c. cake mix
1/4 c. softened margarine
1/2 c. sugar
1 c. pecans

Mix until crumbly; sprinkle on top.
Bake at 350° for 1 hour and 15 minutes. Serve with whipped topping.

Karen Tabor

Quick Cheesecake*

1 (3 oz.) pkg. lemon Jello
3 T. lemon juice
1 (8 oz.) pkg. cream cheese
1 tsp. vanilla
1 c. sugar
1 (12 oz.) can Carnation milk

Dissolve Jello in 1 cup boiling water. Add lemon juice. Cream the sugar and cream cheese. Add vanilla, then add Jello; stir. Whip Carnation milk on high speed until stiff. Slowly add the cream mixture. Make a graham cracker crust using 1/2 pound of graham crackers, crushed, and 1/2 cup butter. Pat on bottom of 9x13-inch pan. Pour cream cheese-Jello mixture over. Chill.
This dessert is light and fluffy and very good after a heavy meal.

Evie Skerik

Hospitality is one form of worship.
The Talmud

Quick Fruit Pie*

1 frozen pie dough in a tin
2 T. flour
1 T. light brown sugar, packed
3 fresh peaches, peeled, halved & pits removed
Juice of 1/2 lemon
3 T. light brown sugar, packed
1 T. unsalted butter, chilled & cubed

Preheat oven to 400°. Place the defrosted pie dough onto a baking sheet and set aside. In a large bowl, mix together 2 tablespoons flour and 1 tablespoon light brown sugar, packed. Toss 3 fresh peaches (peeled, quartered and pits removed), the juice of 1/2 lemon and 3 tablespoons light brown sugar, packed. Toss until peaches are coated. Sprinkle the flour and sugar mixture around the center of the pie crust, leaving a border around the edge. Place peach quarters in the center of the pie crust, leaving a 4-inch border. Sprinkle 1 tablespoon chopped chilled unsalted butter over the peaches. Fold the edges of the dough over the peaches, creasing the dough uniformly. Bake pie at 400° for about 35 minutes. Cover the pie with foil halfway through baking if it is browning too quickly.

Variations: Can also use fresh apples, blueberries, strawberries, pears, etc., or canned apple, cherry, blueberry or mincemeat pie filling.

From: The Forum

Rhubarb Cream Cake*

1 pkg. white or yellow cake mix
4 c. rhubarb, cut up
1 c. sugar
2 c. cream (whipping cream or cultured sour cream)

Prepare cake according to the directions. Pour into a greased and floured 9x13-inch pan. Arrange rhubarb evenly over the top of batter; sprinkle sugar on top of rhubarb. Pour the cream evenly over entire cake mixture. Bake at 350° for 45 to 50 minutes, or until done in the center. Serve warm with whipped cream.

Tastes like a custard rhubarb pie.

If you are lucky to have a great supply of fresh rhubarb, there is so much one can do with it.

Diane Kohler

Rhubarb Pie

1 c. sugar
1/2 tsp. nutmeg
2 eggs, well beaten
3 T. flour
1 T. butter
3 c. rhubarb

Mix together sugar, flour, nutmeg and beaten eggs. Pour over the rhubarb. Bake in double crust for 10 minutes in 400° oven; then turn to 350° for 30 minutes.

Ann Bearfield

Serving Pudding Cone*

This is a great idea for serving food to children.

1 (3 oz.) pkg. instant pudding, any flavor
Milk
1 ice cream cone per person

Prepare pudding as directed on package. Serve in empty ice cream cones. Top with marshmallows and a cherry, if desired. Yield: 6 to 8 servings.

Variations: Potato salad, Jello, pear halves and other foods are fun to serve and eat in ice cream cones.

Kick-the-Can Ice Cream

"Ice cream in a tin can" is my most requested recipe. Homemade ice cream is always the most refreshing dessert, and making it outdoors provides both recreation and a cool, memorable treat. It also creates lifetime memories of fun.

1 (1 lb.) coffee can with plastic lid
1 c. whole milk
1 c. heavy cream
1/3 c. sugar
2 T. flavored syrup (such as chocolate or strawberry)
1 (3 lb.) coffee can with plastic lid, or 1 (No. 10 size) can, such as a potato flake can with plastic lid
Sm. bag ice, cubed (not crushed)
1/2 c. rock salt

In the small can, add milk, cream, sugar and syrup. Do not fill to top. Put lid on small can. Put the small can in the large can. Then put ice and rock salt in layers around the small can. Put lid on large can. Shake for several minutes, until ice cream is ready.

Shaking Ice Cream

MATERIALS:
1 c. whole or low-fat milk
2 T. sugar

1/2 tsp. vanilla extract
4 c. crushed ice
6 T. rock salt

OTHER THINGS YOU'LL NEED:
Measuring cup
Measuring spoons

Pint-size zippable baggie
Gallon-size zippable baggie
4 paper cups & 4 plastic spoons

Help the children to measure 1 cup milk, 2 tablespoons sugar and 1/2 teaspoon vanilla extract into a pint-size zippable baggie. Squeeze out as much air as possible before sealing the baggie. Place the pint-size zippable baggie inside the gallon-size zippable baggie. Add 4 cups crushed ice and 6 tablespoons rock salt to the gallon-size baggie. Squeeze the air out before sealing. Have the children shake the gallon-size baggie vigorously for several minutes. Let them problem-solve about the best way to do this; they may decide to work in teams, take turns individual, wrap the baggie in something to keep their hands from getting too cold, etc. When the ice cream is of the desired consistency, remove the pint-size baggie from the gallon-size baggie and rinse it in clean water to remove the salt. Squeeze the ice cream out of the baggie into the 4 paper cups and serve!

Work is not always required...there is such a thing as sacred idleness, the cultivation of which is now fearfully neglected.
George MacDonald

Sour Cream Cake with Sour Cream Filling

2 eggs, beaten smooth
1 c. sour cream (may use commercial)

Combine.
Put in sifter:
1 c. white sugar
1 1/2 c. flour
1/2 tsp. baking soda
2 tsp. baking powder
Pinch of salt

2 T. cold water
1 tsp. vanilla

Sift together dry ingredients. Add eggs, which have sour cream combined. Add water and vanilla. Bake in 9x9-inch pan at 350° for 30 minutes (until toothpick comes out clean).

FILLING:
1 c. sour cream (commercial may be used)
1 c. white sugar
1 egg

Beat together. Cook over medium heat until boiling and thick. Remove from heat and add 1 teaspoon vanilla and chopped nuts, if desired. Cool and spread on cake. Top with either chocolate or seven-minute frosting.

I received this recipe from the first woman to be a county sheriff in North Dakota, Cecil Livington of Towner, ND. Yes, her name was Cecil – her twin sister was Cecille. She was 70 years old and cooking for the road crew we worked for in 1949. Her husband had been sheriff and when he died, she was appointed and re-elected.

Ruth R. Freund

Smooth and Creamy Frosting*

1 (4-serving size) pkg. instant pudding & pie filling, any flavor
1 c. <u>cold</u> milk
1 (8 oz.) ctn. frozen whipped topping, thawed

Combine pudding mix and milk in a small mixer bowl. Beat on low speed until well blended, about 1 minute. Fold in the whipped topping. Yield: 4 cups or enough to frost two 9-inch layers.
Store frosted cake in the refrigerator.

Coni Horsager

Speedy-Way Cranberry Pudding*

2 c. fresh cranberries, cut in half
1/2 c. molasses
1/2 c. sugar
1 tsp. baking soda
1 1/3 c. flour
1/2 c. hot water

Mix all ingredients and pour into a small microwavable bundt pan that has been sprayed with vegetable shortening. Microwave about 6 minutes on FULL POWER, or until done, turning every 2 minutes. Let cool slightly. Then turn out of pan. Can be served warm with Butter Sauce or frozen for later use.

BUTTER SAUCE:
1/2 c. cream
1/2 c. butter
1 c. sugar

Microwave 3 minutes, stirring every minute. Serve warm on Cranberry Pudding. Sauce can be reheated.

Gwen Fraase

7-Up Apple Dumplings

2 c. sugar
1 tsp. cinnamon
1/2 tsp. nutmeg
1 stick butter
20 oz. 7-Up
10 lg. apples
1 can biscuits
1/4 c. sugar
1 tsp. nutmeg
1 tsp. cinnamon
1/2 stick butter

In saucepan, combine first group of sugar, cinnamon, nutmeg, butter and 7-Up. Heat until melted; set aside. Peel and core apples, separate dough from 1 can biscuits. Separate and roll out each biscuit individually and place 1 apple in each. Combine second group of sugar, cinnamon and nutmeg. Sprinkle 1 teaspoon of this mixture in center of each apple along with 2 teaspoons butter. Fold biscuit around apple and pinch dough. Put dumplings in 9x13-inch pan. Pour sauce over each dumpling. Bake at 375° for 45 minutes.

LaVira Eggermont

Life itself is the proper binge.
Julia Child

Strawberry Angel Delight*

1 angel food cake
1 (6 oz.) pkg. strawberry Jello
2 (10 oz.) pkg. frozen strawberries
(do not thaw)
1 (8 oz.) ctn. Cool Whip

Prepare angel food cake following the box. Break angel food cake into small pieces. Put half of the cake pieces into a 9x13-inch pan. Mix Jello with 1 1/2 cups hot water until dissolved. Add frozen strawberries. Stir to thaw. When all dissolved and Jello starts to gel, fold in Cool Whip. Pour 1/2 of strawberry mixture over broken pieces of cake. Add other half of cake pieces. Pour remaining strawberry mixture over cake pieces. Refrigerate.

Kristen Lindgren

Flops are a part of life's menu and I am never a girl to miss out on a course.
Rosalind Russell

Strawberry Cheesecake Squares With Gingersnap Crust

CRUST:
2 c. gingersnap crumbs (about 36 gingersnap cookies)
1/3 c. (5 1/3 T.) butter, melted

FILLING:
4 c. stemmed strawberries (about 1 1/4 lb.)
3 (8 oz.) pkg. cream cheese, softened
1 c. powdered sugar
1 tsp. vanilla extract
1 (8 oz.) ctn. frozen whipped topping, thawed (see note)
1 (1/4 oz.) env. unflavored gelatin
1/3 c. cold water

OPTIONAL GARNISH:
Additional frozen whipped topping, thawed
Whole strawberries
Sugar

Crust: In medium bowl, combine gingersnap crumbs and butter, mixing until blended. Press onto bottom of 9x13-inch baking pan; cover and refrigerate.

Filling: In blender or food processor container, process strawberries into a smooth sauce; set aside. In mixer bowl, beat together cream cheese, sugar and vanilla until blended. Stir in whipped topping. In small saucepan, sprinkle gelatin over water; let stand 1 minute. Heat over low heat until gelatin is completely dissolved, stirring occasionally. Add 1 1/4 cups of the strawberry sauce, stirring to blend. Using a rubber spatula, fold strawberry-gelatin mixture into cream cheese mixture. Pour onto prepared crust. Cover and refrigerate until firm, about 4 hours or overnight.

To serve, cut into 20 squares. Garnish tops with additional whipped topping and strawberries, if desired. Serve with remaining strawberry sauce (sweeten sauce with sugar if necessary). Yield: 20 servings.

Note: For a lower-fat version, substitute reduced-fat cream cheese and reduced-fat whipped topping for regular cream cheese and whipped topping. Proceed as recipe directs.

From: The Forum

Beauty is an ecstasy; it is as simple as hunger.
W. Somerset Maugham

Strawberry Frosting*

1 (8 oz.) ctn. frozen whipped topping, thawed (can be fat-free)
1 (4-serving size) box strawberry Jello
1 box frozen strawberries, thawed

Place strawberries with juice into a large mixer bowl. Mix for 1 minute to crush strawberries. Add the dry Jello and continue to beat until the Jello is dissolved. Slowly mix in the whipped topping. Cover the bowl with plastic wrap and chill for 1/2 hour.

Yield: enough to generously frost an angel food cake that has been chilled or frozen.

Keeps well, covered, in the refrigerator.

Variation: Raspberries and raspberry Jello can be used, which is excellent on a chocolate 9x13-inch sheet cake.

Coni Horsager

Strawberry Pie*

PIE CRUST:
1 1/2 c. flour
1 tsp. salt
1 tsp. sugar

Sift into 9-inch pie tin. Make a well in flour.

Pour into well:
1/2 c. Crisco oil
2 T. milk

Press with fingers in pie pan. Bake 15 to 20 minutes at 350°. Cool.

STRAWBERRY PIE FILLING:
1 3/4 c. water
2 T. cornstarch
1 c. sugar

Cook until clear, 1 minute.
Add:
1 (3 oz.) pkg. strawberry Jello
Pinch of salt
1 tsp. vanilla
1 T. butter
1 qt. strawberries

Pour into baked shell and refrigerate.

Arla Kapaun

Strawberry Shortcut Cake

1 c. mini marshmallows
2 (10 oz.) pkg. frozen, sliced strawberries, in syrup, thawed
1 (3 oz.) pkg. strawberry gelatin
1 1/2 c. sugar
1/2 c. solid shortening
3 eggs
2 1/4 c. flour
3 tsp. baking powder
1/2 tsp. salt
1 c. milk
1 tsp. vanilla

Generously grease bottom only of 9x13-inch pan; sprinkle marshmallows evenly over bottom of pan. Combine thawed strawberries and syrup with dry gelatin; thoroughly mix and set aside. Combine remaining ingredients; blend at low speed until moistened. Beat at medium speed 3 minutes, scraping sides of bowl occasionally. Pour batter evenly over marshmallows in pan. Spoon strawberry mixture evenly over batter. Bake at 350° for 45 to 50 minutes, or until done and golden brown. Serve warm or cool with ice cream or whipped cream.

*Mrs. F.S.,
Sargent Co. ND*

Swedish Apple Pie*

6 to 8 sliced apples
1 T. sugar
1 tsp. cinnamon
1/2 c. melted butter
1 egg
1 c. sugar
3/4 c. flour
1/2 c. pecans

In pie pan or 8x8-inch pan, place sliced apples. Sprinkle 1 tablespoon sugar and 1 teaspoon cinnamon mixture over top. Mix together melted butter, egg, 1 cup sugar, flour and pecans; spread over apples. Bake at 350° for 55 minutes.
This crustless pie is so easy to make and so---good!

*Marian Gerntholz ,
Eleanor Martinson*

*Age does not diminish the extreme disappointment
of having a scoop of ice cream fall from the cone.
Jim Fiebig*

Swedish Nut Cake*

2 c. sugar
2 c. flour
2 eggs
1/2 tsp. baking soda
1 (20 oz.) can crushed pineapple, including juice
1/2 c. chopped nuts
1 c. brown sugar
1/2 stick margarine, softened
1 (8 oz.) pkg. cream cheese, softened
Nuts, for topping

Preheat oven to 350°. Mix sugar, flour, eggs, baking soda, pineapple and juice in a mixing bowl. Add 1/2 cup nuts and pour into a 9x12x2-inch greased baking pan. Bake 40 minutes.

For frosting, mix brown sugar, margarine and cream cheese in a bowl. Spread on cake while it is hot. Sprinkle with nuts.

Note: Have margarine and cream cheese at room temperature before making frosting.

From: American Profile

Triple Citrus Cheesecake

FILLING:
4 (8 oz.) pkg. Philadelphia cream cheese, softened
1 c. granulated sugar
2 T. flour
1 tsp. vanilla
1 T. fresh lemon juice

CRUST:
1 c. Honey Maid graham cracker crumbs

1 T. lime juice
1 T. orange juice
1 tsp. grated lemon peel
1 tsp. grated lime peel
1 tsp. grated orange peel
4 eggs
1/3 c. firmly-packed brown sugar
1/4 c. (1/2 stick) butter or margarine, melted

Crust: Mix crumbs, brown sugar and butter or margarine; press onto bottom of 9-inch springform pan. Bake at 325° for 10 minutes if using a silver springform pan (bake at 300° for 10 minutes if using a dark nonstick springform pan).

Filling: Mix cream cheese, granulated sugar, flour and vanilla with electric mixer on medium speed until well blended. Blend in juices and peels. Add eggs, one at a time, mixing on low speed after each addition just until blended. Pour over crust.

Bake at 325° for 60 to 65 minutes, or until center is almost set if using silver springform pan (bake at 300° for 60 to 65 minutes, or until center is almost set if using a dark nonstick springform pan). Run knife or metal spatula around rim of pan to loosen cake; cool before removing rim of pan. Refrigerate 4 hours or overnight. Yield: 12 servings.

From: Philadelphia Cream Cheese ad

Yvette's Pumpkin Dessert

4 eggs
1 sm. can pumpkin
1 1/2 c. sugar
3 1/2 tsp. pumpkin pie spice
2 c. evaporated milk

Mix.

1 yellow cake mix

Take out 1 cup of cake mix and set aside, dry. To rest of cake mix, add 1 stick oleo, melted. Spread in greased 9x13-inch pan. Pour pumpkin mix over.

To the 1 cup of cake mix, add:

1/4 c. sugar
1/4 c. soft oleo
1 tsp. cinnamon
1/4 c. nuts (opt.)

Crumble over top and bake at 350° for 50 to 60 minutes. Cool. Top with whipped cream.

Very good!

Candy Odegaard

Notes & Recipes

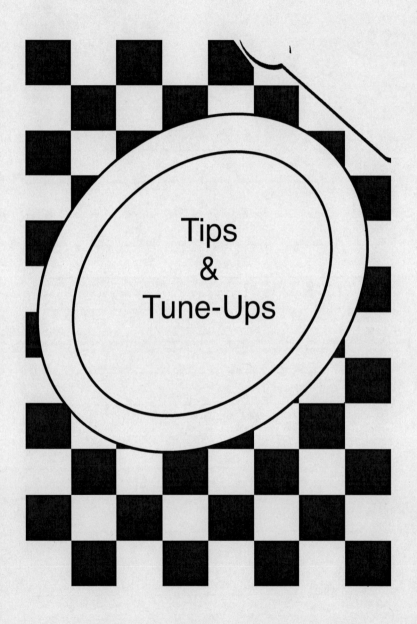

Notes & Recipes

Tips & Tune-Ups

In The Kitchen

Use a wood and metal pant holder (hanger) to hold open your recipe book when you are cooking. Can be hung from a cupboard knob at eye level for easy viewing. (Today Show)

Use a pastry blender to break up ground beef while browning. Pastry blender is also good for slicing cold, hard-boiled eggs.

What to do when you are out of butter: 2 cups of evaporated milk, beaten slowly, will turn into a pound of butter. Pour into a pan and chill. Salt may be added. (Ardys)

Want to keep recipe cards clean? Put a clear pie plate over the card while mixing. If you are using a cookbook, it will also help keep the page open to your page. (Ardys)

Add 3 chicken bouillon cubes to Bean Soup for extra flavor. (Marcy)

Strawberries stay fresh longer if they are stored in a colander in the refrigerator. The colander allows the cold air to circulate between the berries. (Ardys)

To get rid of fruit flies, set vinegar out in a jar. The pests will head straight to the jar and drown. (Carol)

If you need a substitute for a square of unsweetened chocolate in a recipe, use 3 tablespoons cocoa powder and 1 tablespoon of solid vegetable shortening. (Heloise)

When baking a homemade cake, add 2 tablespoons boiling water to the butter and sugar mixture. This will make a finer-textured cake. (Ardys)

Use Lifesavers for birthday candle holders. Those in the rolls are the right size. The ones in a bag are larger and don't work as well. (REAL SIMPLE Magazine)

If a recipe calls for melted shortening, melt it in your baking pan while the oven preheats. You then have shortening in the pan to grease and flour it, and you also save time having to wash an extra cup or pan used for melting. (Ardys)

Use cooking spray on measuring cups to keep peanut butter from sticking. It slides right out. (Carol)

Before boiling potatoes, rice, pasta or eggs: Rub margarine or spray Pam around the top inside of the kettle. It keeps it from boiling over. (Carol)

Lemons heated before squeezing will give twice the quantity of juice. (Christine, Carol)

For a small child's room, use pictures for labels on drawers or boxes.

To clean your microwave, heat a bowl of water on HIGH for 5 to 10 minutes. Keep the bowl in the oven for several minutes more, so the steam can do the cleaning for you. Remove the bowl of water carefully and then wipe the oven walls and top with a clean cloth. Easy, without any effort.

Use coffee filters (flatten, the round, pleated kind) placed between plates, bowls, glassware to cushion and prevent rattling. (Ann)

Coffee filters are good for children's art projects, using water colors. (Ann)

To prepare a mango, wash fruit. Hold flat-side down in the palm of your left hand. Score the skin with a sharp knife around the outside perimeter. Peel only the top half. Slice both horizontal and vertical cuts straight down to the pit. The size slices you want determines the number of cuts. Now, you can cut across the flat side of the pit to remove the slices you have made. Turn over to peel and slice the other half. (Janice)

After washing leaf lettuce, drain in colander. Store in a zip-lock bag with 2 to 3 white paper towels. This will remove the excess moisture. Do not tear leaves until ready for use. (Janice)

Quick and easy way to clean the George Foreman grill: After removing grilled food, unplug and place a damp cloth on the bottom grill and bring the top down. While you are eating, the grill will steam clean and it only takes a quick wipe up afterwards. (Marcella)

When peeling apples for pie or salad, first pour a cup or more of cider into a bowl, then drop the cut up apple slices in as you continue to peel more. When you have the amount needed, drain slices in colander...pieces will remain white and the cider enhances the taste. (Marcella)

One helpful hint that I have never seen in any book is: When cooking beans or cabbage, add a tablespoon of vinegar to eliminate the tendency to produce "gas". This is an old German trick! (Norma)

When canning dill pickles, put a carrot stick or two in each jar. Yummy! (Carol)

A dish of vanilla in the refrigerator will remove odors. (Carol)

After shredding cheese, sprinkle it with a little flour and shake. The shredded cheese will not stick together and can be stored in the refrigerator for later use. (Carol)

Dip bacon in cold water before frying to prevent curling. (Carol)

Do not put tomatoes in the sun or on the windowsill to ripen. Instead, put in warm dark places. Store with the stems pointed downward and they will retain their freshness. (Carol)

If the end of your Scotch tape sticks to the roll, refrigerate it. In 10 minutes, it can be pried up without breaking the tape. (Carol)

Cut onions at the top instead of root to prevent them from burning your eyes. Or hold a stick match sticking out of your mouth and the sulphur in the match head will help to keep your eyes from burning. (Carol)

A teaspoon of vinegar added to the water in which eggs are poached keeps the whites from spreading. (Carol)

An old toothbrush is a good cleaning tool. It can get into difficult plates to reach. (Carol)

Wax candles burn longer if chilled thoroughly in the refrigerator before lighting. (Carol)

Put a few drops of oil of peppermint in your hot dishwasher to make your kitchen smell nice.

When breading chicken, try coating the pieces with mayonnaise instead of egg. The mayonnaise clings to the chicken and doesn't drip off like the egg does. Plus, it adds a nice flavor. (Carol)

If your homemade soup gets too salty, add a potato or two to tone down the salty taste. (Carol)

To soften rock hard brown sugar, put it in a microwave-safe dish with a slice of apple. Cover and heat for 15 to 20 seconds. Let stand 5 minutes. Remove apple and break up the sugar with a fork.

Add raw rice to the salt shaker to keep salt free-flowing.

Hungry for a BLT and there's no bacon in the house? Use Bac-Os (bits), spreading generously over the tomato and lettuce layers. (Helen)

Good dried beef, like that made at Valley Meat Supply in Valley City, makes a better BLT than bacon ever did! (Marcella)

Banana bread, toasted, is delicious. (Helen)

Around the House

HOMEMADE FURNITURE STRIP:
1 pt. warm water   **1 T. cornstarch**
1 T. Lewis lye

Stir until thick, brush on painted surface. Let work a short time. Scrape or brush off. Don't leave on surface too long. (Ardys)

For ring around the collar: Apply Prell shampoo before putting into the washer. (Marcella)

To remove stubborn stains on washable clothing, use Dial Liquid hand soap on spot, before washing. (Marcella)

Pam cooking spray can be used in an emergency to correct squeaks in door hinges, door knobs, furniture, sliding door rails.

Use a comb to hold a nail in place while you hammer it into the walls. (From: Women's Day magazine)

Put a clothespin at the end of a retractable vacuum cord to keep from rewinding before you want it to.

If the nozzle of the hairspray can gets clogged, tip the can over in a tall glass of water overnight.

To thread a needle easily, cut the thread on the bias (slant). (Christine)

To clean silver, put foil in the bottom of a cake pan. Add hot water, salt and a little water-softener. Place silverware in the hot water until it is no longer stained. (Today Show, 1/24/04)

To remove marks on floor tile or covering, use toothpaste and gently brush. (Haley's Hints, Today Show)

If zipper sticks, run a bar of soap over the teeth or turn a lead pencil over the teeth and it will glide easily. (Carol)

Clean around kitchen faucets with white vinegar. Just pour on and wipe clean. (Vi)

To keep celery fresh and crisp longer, clean and wrap in foil and store in the refrigerator. Foil stays colder than plastic containers or wrap. (Shirley)

Pierce hard avocado and put in microwave for 20 seconds, then test for softness. Microwave until avocado has softened and is ready to use. (Sharon)

When you bring celery home from the produce department, wash it and cut up. Chop up all the cleaned leaves and short tops and bag; freeze for a later time when soup is on the menu. (Clarice)

Chop celery leaves and some small stalks, add a little water and a dash of salt and microwave all for about 30 seconds. Let cool and freeze in a zip-lock bag for later use in soup or casserole. (Marcy)

Leave potato chips in their original bag and freeze. They won't get soggy and will stay fresh for unexpected company. (Marcy)

Freeze clean, washed green or red seedless grapes for a quick snack or last minute addition to a fruit salad.

If you have different cereals that are almost gone, make Rice Krispie bars...any cereal work well and a mixture is even more interesting.

Keep a notepad and pencil on a string, attached near the telephone for messages. The attached pen will not "walk away".

If a cracked dish is boiled for 45 minutes in sweet milk, the crack will be so welded together that it will hardly be visible and will be so strong it will stand the same usage as before. (Leona)

To clean WHITE bleachable socks (not silk or rayon), mix 1/4 cup liquid chlorine beach and 1 cup powdered dishwasher detergent and 1 gallon of hot water, mixing until all soap powder is dissolved. Use a plastic, enamel or stainless-steel container, or your kitchen sink. If the material can't take hot water, let it cool. Let the socks soak for 5 to 10 minutes. Rinse well and then wash as usual. (Heloise)

Stacking cake layers is easier if you let the cake cool and slice the rounded top off with a serrated knife. If there are 3 layers, the top layer could be left domed.

To "pipe" filling into deviled eggs, place the filling in a resealable plastic bag and snip off a corner of the bag. Then you can pipe directly into the egg whites. Can be used for decorating cookies or cakes, too, after the basic frosting is in place. (Mr. Food)

To remove pet hair from clothing or furniture, use a rubber glove and wipe it off. A damp sponge also removes pet hair from furniture cushions.

A foggy bathroom mirror can be easily cleaned using shaving cream and paper towels.

To revitalize wood furniture or antiques, use equal parts of linseed oil, white vinegar and turpentine. Rub into the furniture or wood with a soft cloth and lots of elbow grease.

Drop lemons into very hot water before squeezing and they will hold more juice. (Christine)

Slow kitchen drain? Put 2 or 3 tablespoons of soft mechanics hand soap in the drain and then run a small amount of water and let it set overnight. The soap will dissolve the grease. (Christine)

To keep deer away from flowers: Mix 1 egg into 1 quart of water, add lots of garlic powder. Put into a spray bottle and coat your plants. (Christine)

To keep your fresh ground meat free of harmful bacteria, add 1 teaspoon onion or garlic powder and 1 teaspoon pureed prunes per pound of meat.

Get a great shine on chrome fixtures and mirrors by using rubbing alcohol applied with a soft cloth or cotton balls. Use a "retired" toothbrush to clean around faucets, shower door tracks.

If you have trouble putting on a clasp bracelet by yourself, place a small piece of tape across one end of the bracelet and tape it to your wrist. Bring the other end and close the clasp. (Woman's Day magazine)

Health

Sinus Prevention Recipe: 1 quart warm water, 2 teaspoons pickling salt (not table salt), 1 teaspoon baking soda. When sinus headache starts, mix all and put in a squeeze bottle, which has a tube. Lean back and put tube into nostril, pour all in and be prepared to sneeze! Spray lightly for general stuffiness.

A pinch of ginger in 1/4 cup warm water settles your stomach. (Marian)

Eat sour cherries and the juice, the acid helps to relieve the grout. (Irma)
Put some whiskey in the ear to help an earache. (Old wives tale)

Ice water in the ear will help get out an insect. (Old wives tale)

Relief for croup: Take a wool sock or cloth and put it in ice cold water. Wring it out and wrap it around the throat. Then, take another wool scarf or cloth and wrap it around the cold one. Repeat this about every 15 minutes. (Otie)

To rid any toenails of nail fungus, trim the affected nail and rub with Vicks Vapo-Rub twice a day. The Vicks acts on the new nail growth, so results may take a couple months as toenails are slow growing. (From a column by Dr. Gott)

Feeling insecure in certain situation? Pause. Slowly turn your head from side to side, left to right. Helps to balance your equilibrium. (Carole)

Using cinnamon generously in the diet is especially good for diabetics... cinnamon has good medicinal properties. (From research at Human Nutrition Research Center, MD)

For a sore throat: Mix 1 to 2 teaspoons salt into glass of warm water. Gargle, as long, and as often as you can. My mother's advice for all sore throats. Don't know why, but it seems to work! (Colleen, advice from Cathy)

Outdoors

Pancakes at camp will be lighter if you use club soda instead of water. Use up all the batter, as it will go flat. (Ardys)

When aphids strike, spray plants weekly with a solution of 1 1/2 teaspoons baking soda to 1 pint of water.

Aluminum foil over the top of cooked camp foods keeps food hot in cool area until everyone gathers around the picnic table. Good especially for biscuits. (Ardys)

Want to travel with eggs, break enough for scrambled eggs in a fruit jar and seal, put in cooler, easy to mix with milk and bacon (precooked and chopped) the next morning at the camp site. Don't forget oil/frying pan, salt and pepper. (Ardys)

Leftover mashed potatoes can be made into patties, coat with flour for potato pancakes, flash-freeze, then store in Zip-lock freezer bags. Take along for camping trip in cooler, fry in oil. (Ardys)

Camping Tips for Busy Moms or Den Mothers: When my kids were little, and we tented, I would use loaf bread bags (zip-locks now available) to put in one-day's clothes (shorts, t-shirt, underpants and socks, or jeans, shirt, sock and underpants). I could store 7 days of clothing in a small travel bag with side pockets or books, games, clean shoes, bath kit. At the end of the day, they put on pajamas and put that day's dirty clothes in the day's bread bag. This method kept the floor of the tent neat, clothes clean and dirty clothes away from clean clothes until we could get to a Laundromat. (Ardys H.)

DECK WASH RECIPE:
2 gal. water
2 c. bleach
1 c. dishwashing detergent
(powder)

I use this in an electric floor scrubber with bristle brushes, rinse well. This is good to use before putting on a new wood deck stain. (Ardys Horner)

*Life is not measured by the number of breaths we take,
but by the moments that take our breath away.*

Potion for Deskunking the Dog

1 qt. hydrogen peroxide   1 tsp. soap (dishwashing soap)
1/4 c. baking soda

Mix together in a pail. Give dog a bath with the whole batch. Repeat as often as necessary!
This really works! (Kevin)

List of My Favorite Condiments

Tuong To Sriracha Hot Chili Sauce from Huy Fong Foods, Rosemead, CA (626) 286-8328 www.huyfong.com. This stuff is good on almost anything, I won't eat eggs without it.

Tuong To Toi Viet Nam Chili Garlic Sauce from Huy Fong Foods, Rosemead, CA (626) 286-8328 www.huyfong.com. Great flavor, but use this stuff carefully, it actually is hot.

Veri Veri Teriyaki from Soy Vayx, Felton, CA (800) 600-2077 www.soyvay.com. Amazing flavor, best on fish, but also good on chicken and meat.

La Victoria Red Taco Sauce from Authentic Specialty Foods, Chino, CA (800) 725-9705 www.lavictoria.com. Really good traditional taco sauce.

Near East Brand Couscous - A great alternative to rice or potatoes and cooks up fast.

Diamond Crystal Kosher Salt - For some reason this stuff makes poultry and meat more tender and flavorful.

HP Sauce – This is a British sauce that's great on steaks and sausages.

Dijon Mustard – Kind of goes without saying, but you can't live without this stuff. Good for sandwiches, burgers, or chicken or to mix up a quick Dijon vinaigrette salad dressing.

Paul Newman Brand salad dressings – Good stuff!

Pepperidge Farm Italian croutons. (Tom)

Hunger is the best seasoning.
Swedish proverb

Something Special Added...

Savory Sandwiches: Keep a custard cup of chopped fresh parsley in the refrigerator to sprinkle on sandwiches made with deli meats, cheese, egg salad, tuna salad or salmon salad to enhance the flavor.

Apple Pie: When making apple pie, use 3 parts white to 1 part brown sugar and add pumpkin pie spice instead of cinnamon and nutmeg.

Banana Bread: Stir in cut-up dried apricots, dried pineapple pieces and candied red and green cherries. Your banana bread becomes very special.

Mashed Potatoes: If there is any spinach dip left over after a party, mix it into a batch of mashed potatoes. Yum.

Chicken Breasts: Add flavor by marinating uncooked chicken breasts overnight in bottled salad dressing. Or, once the chicken has been cooked, spoon on some barbecue sauce, sprinkle on herbs; squeeze a little lemon juice over meat or top with salsa, relish, pesto or chutney.

Brownies: Baking brownies from a mix, try using half of the water called for on the box and make up the difference with raspberry syrup. It makes the brownies very moist and gives an added flavor.

Instant Coffee: Mix in vanilla extract and vanilla-flavored nondairy creamer. It will taste like store-bought specialty coffee.

Baked Beans: Improve canned baked beans with ketchup, diced onion and brown sugar; add a bit of cinnamon.

Meat Loaf: To perk up meat loaf, grind up Bugles snack or flavored potato chips and add them instead of bread crumbs.

Veggies: When cooking peas and carrots, add a small amount of honey to the cooking water.

From: Highline Notes, May 2003

When preparing bacon, lay slices in a 10x15-inch bar pan, put in a 400° oven, uncovered, for 10 minutes, or until crisp. Lay on paper towel to blot excess fat. Using clean paper towel, lay in single layer, roll up and place in baggy. Bacon is ready for use as needed, without frying each time a recipe calls for a couple slices. (I always cut each slice in half before placing in pan to bake.) (Pauline)

Success is the only thing some people cannot forgive in a friend.

By her own admission, Marcella Richman is an addicted recipe collector, in search of a support group! The beginning step to her recovery was to compile and edit the accumulated treasures into book form. Now, ten years later, this is the third in her series of cookbooks launched from her home-based business, North Dakota Cookbooks.

Married to Wayne Richman, she is the mother of Ann and Amanda, mother-in-law to Kevin, and grandmother to Brett and Allison. She has a Bachelor of Science degree from Valley City (ND) State University and a Master of Liberal Arts degree from Minnesota State University, Moorhead.

Aside from a life-long love of writing, she counts music, golf, travel, reading and cooking as recreational outlets.

Notes & Recipes

Index

Start Your Engines – Appetizers, Snacks & Drinks

Adult Root Beer Floats
Almond Candy
Artichoke Dip 1
Buttermilk Shake
Candied Pecans
Caramel Popcorn
Chocolate Fudge 2
Cinnamon Trail Mix
Crab Dip
Crab-Filled Mini Popovers 3
Cranberry Trail Mix
Cream Cheese Roll-Ups
Crispy Cheese Crackers 4
Broiled Crab Melt-Aways
Delicious Shrimp Dip
Deviled Eggs with Sour Cream
    And Salmon Roe 5
Don's Popcorn Balls
Dreamy Fruit Dip
Easy Homemade Freezer Jam
Easy Way Pizza Rolls 6
Fairway Fuel
Fast Fudge
Green Olive Cheese Ball 7
Grilled Tuna Sandwich
Hot Reuben Dip
Hot Spinach Artichoke Dip 8
Ice Cream Fudge
Easy Marble Bark
Jutta's Easy Dip 9
Mexican Artichoke Dip
Millionaire's Candy 10
Microwave Caramel Corn
Nacho Sauce
North Dakota Guacamole 11
Olive-Ham Cheese Ball
Orange Julius
Orange Popsicle Drink 12
Oriental Chicken Wings
Party Cheese Ball
Party Meat Balls 13
Party Pretzels
Peanut Sauce
Pepper Pots
Pizza on a Bun 14
Pizza Sandwich
Quick Bar-B-Que Sauce
Red Pepper Cheese Ball
Refried Bean Dip 15
Rhubarb Slush
Reuben Hot Dip
Salmon Dip 16
Seven Wives Inn Granola
Simply Surprising Dip
Shrimp Dip Deluxe 17
Skinny Vegetable Dip
Snack Mix
Snowmints 18
Snowman Soup
Stuffed Mushrooms
Sugar and Spice Snacks 19
Strawberry Freezer Jam
Summertime Fruit Slush
Tex-Mex Dip 20
Texas Trash
Toffee
Tropical Fruit Dip/Fruit Butter 21
Sangria
Summer Slush
Sweet Pickles from Dill
    Pickles 22
Tortilla Roll-Ups
Triscuit Nachos
Turkey Taco Dip 23
Veggie Sandwich
Water Chestnuts in Bacon
    and Sauce
White Italian Sangria 24
White Sangria 25

Brake for Breads & Brunch

Almond-Poppy Seed Bread
Apple Oatmeal Breakfast
    Cookies 27
Apple-Sausage French Toast
Bacon 'N' Egg Tacos 28
Baked Cinnamon Bread Custard

Blueberry French Toast 29
Breakfast in a Glass
Breakfast Fritters
Breakfast Casserole 30
Breakfast Pizza
Breakfast Soufflé
Brunch Cheesecake 31
Buttermilk Nut Bread
Cheddar Biscuits 32
Cherry Cream Crescents
Chocolate Banana Bread
Cinnamon Pastries 33
Cocoa Muffins
Cottage Cheese Scrambled Eggs
Cream Bread 34
Dole Pineapple Berry Smoothie
Dutch Babies
Easy Cornbread (or Muffins) 35
Egg Sausage Soufflé
Friendship Bread
Fruit Fizz 36
Jiffy Cinnamon Rolls 37
Healthy Apple-Walnut Muffins
Hot Curried Fruit 38
Italian Bread
Jamaican Banana Bread 39
Jiffy Cornbread Bake
Lazy Man's Rolls
Maple Breakfast Rolls.................. 40
Never-Fail Buns
No-Knead Dark Bread
Nutmeg Sour Cream Muffins 41
Oatmeal Rolls 42
Ole's Swedish Hot Cakes 43
One-Pan Applesauce-Raisin
  Coffeecake
Orange-Nut Bread 44
Orange Peach Smoothies
Orange Pull-Apart Bread
Overnight Omelet 45
Pecan Orange Muffins
Pecan Pie Muffins 46
Pumpkin Maple Cream Cheese
  Muffins
Quiche I 47
Quiche II
Rich Pumpkin Coffeecake 48

Scandinavian Cinnamon Rolls
  or Coffeecakes 49
Secret to Southern Cornbread
Simply Coffeecake 50
Sourdough Biscuits
Stormy Day Breakfast Bread
  Pudding 51
Super Quick Sticky Caramel
  Rolls
Swiss Onion Loaf 52
Tex-Mex Biscuits
Tinnicci's Coffeecake 53
Tortillas and Eggs
Travis' Mexican Omelette
Yellow Bread 54
Zucchini Oatmeal Muffins
Zucchini Pancakes 55

Speedway Salads & Sides

Ada's Black Cherry Jello
Almond-Orange Salad 57
Apricot Salad
Avocado Egg Salad
Avocado-Tomato Salad 58
Balkan Cucumber Salad
Baked Cranberry Sauce
Broccoli Peanut Salad 59
Champagne Fruit Bowl
Cherry Dessert or Salad
Chicken-Rice Salad 60
Coleslaw
Cranberry Chutney
Cranberry Mold 61
Crunchy Coleslaw I
Crunchy Coleslaw II
Deluxe Scalloped Corn 62
Easy Egg Salad
Fast Fruit Salad
Festive Carrot-Apple Salad 63
Fudge-Stripe Salad
Grape Chicken Salad
Green Beans with Bacon 64
Green Treasure Salad
Grilled Chicken and Fruit Salad
"Health" Salad 65
Honey-Mustard Dressing

Hot Chicken Salad
Lettuce-Fruit Salad 66
Lettuce Salad
Lime Hershey Salad
Lime Salad................................... 67
Mandarin Salad
Melon Salad................................. 68
Old-time Fruit Salad
Oven Orange-Glazed Carrots
Poppy Seed Dressing.................. 69
Poppy Seed Dressing
Potato Pancakes for Two
Pizza Salad................................. 70
Quickie Chickie Salad
Fruit and Cookie Salad
Rose's Salad 71
Betty's Salmon Salad
Shrimp Louie
Simple Summer Salad
Snicker Bar Salad....................... 72
Southwest Pasta Salad
Sparkling Fruit Salad
Sunny Summer Tomato Salad
Sunshine Salad 73
Super Strawberry Lettuce
Swiss Vegetable Medley
Tropical Chicken Salad................ 74
Vinaigrette Dressing
Zucchini with Zip......................... 75

Put the Pedal to the Kettle – Meats & Main Dishes

Aggie's Enchilada Casserole....... 77
Bacon-Wrapped Chicken
Baked Halibut
Baked Potato Soup..................... 78
Bar-B-Q Chicken
BBQ Beef and Pork
Bar-B-Q Oven Meat Balls........... 79
Barbecued Spare Ribs
Beef Stroganoff Sandwich
Beef Taco Bake 80
Belgian Pork with Sauerkraut
Best-Ever Meat Loaf................... 81
Black Bean Soup
Brett's Chicken and Herb Casserole
Broccoli-Cheese Casserole......... 82
Bubble Pizza
Cake Pan Potatoes..................... 83
Carol's One-Step Lasagna
Cheeseburger Bake.................... 84
Cheeseburger Soup
Cheesy Vegetable Soup.............. 85
Chicken Casserole (2)................ 86
Chicken Cutlets with Couscous
    And Toasted Pine Nuts
Chicken with Biscuits.................. 87
Chicken Enchilada Soup
Chicken Huntington
Chicken Parmesan 88
Chicken Salad Tacos
Chicken Quesadillas
Chicken Tortilla Soup.................. 89
Chicken Tortilla Soup
Cincinnati Chili Soup
Cola Chicken 90
Cottage Cheese Pocket Recipe
Crab Alfredo
Creamed Chicken....................... 91
Easy Chicken A La King
Make It Easy Chicken................. 92
Chili Verde
Crock-Pot Beef Stew
Cruise Control Pork
    Tenderloin 93
Easy Hot Dish
Fake Lasagna............................. 94
Foolproof Swiss Steak
Forgotten Chicken
Four-Minute Dumplings 95
Garlicky Chicken Breasts
Garrison Keillor's Family Meat
    Loaf.. 96
General Tso's Chicken
Grandma's Delicious Swiss
    Steak with Dumplings 97
Grand Slam Chili
Gourmet Tomato Soup 98
Hamburger Dill Casserole
High Hat...................................... 99
Honey-Lemon Chicken
Italian Meat Loaf Pie................... 100

Italian Subs
Lentil Soup 101
Linguine with Garlic Clam
  Sauce
Mexican Lasagna 102
Microwave Orange Roughy
Minted Meat Balls 103
Nancy's Corn, Cheese,
  Green Chili Pie
No-Peel Potato Casserole
Oatmeal Meat Loaf 104
Pantry Pasta
Peasant-Style Chicken 105
Pheasant (Chicken) Dumpling
  Soup
Pizza Meat Loaf 106
Pizza Casserole
Pork Chop Ramen
Potato Boats 107
Potato Pepperoni Hot Dish
Quick Cabbage Soup
Quick-Into-The-Oven
  Casserole 108
Quick Pork Chops Over Stuffing
Ranch Potatoes
Randy's Chili 109
Rasta Pasta
Roadside Potatoes 110
Russian River Chicken 111
Salisbury Steak
Sauerkraut Casserole
Scalloped Potatoes 112
Seafood Casserole
Seafood Jubilee
Simple Chicken 113
Skillet Barbecued Pork Chops
Sloppy Joes
Slow-Cooker Winter Vegetable
  Soup 114
Souper Enchiladas
Speedy Rice Krispie Hot Dish
Supreme Lasagna 115
Surprise Cheese Burgers
Taco Soup 116
Tasty BBQ Pork Chops
Teriyaki Pork Roast 117
Teriyaki Salmon with Red
  Potatoes
Tina's Cheesy Potato Bake 118
Tortellini and Bean Soup
Tortilla Soup 119
Turkey Burgers
Turkey Sausage
Tuscan White Bean Soup 120
X-Tra Good Vegetable Soup 121

Fuel Stop – Cookies & Bars

Almond Cookies 123
Almond-Glazed Sugar
  Cookies 124
Best Brownies
Best Oatmeal Cookies
Candy Cane Snowballs 125
Caramel-Nut Wedges
Cashew Cookies 126
Carrot Bars
Chocolate Chip Bars
Chocolate-Chocolate
  Brownies 127
Chocolate Cookie Treats
Chocolate-Peanut-Heath
  Cookie 128
Thick, Soft and Chewy
  Chocolate Chip Cookies 129
Thin, Crispy Chocolate Chip
  Cookies 130
Coconut-Pecan Cookies
Chocolate Pecan Shortbread
  Cookies 131
Cream Cheese Cookies
Cream Cheese German
  Chocolate Cake Bars
Cute Christmas "Cookie" 132
Cut-Out Sugar Cookies
Date Cookies 133
Deluxe Chocolate-Marshmallow
  Bars
Drumsticks 134
Easy Coconut Brownies
Favorite Dump Bars
"Freckles" 135
Haystacks
Joel's "One" Cookies 136

Joe's Peanut Bars
Lemon Bars
Mixed Nut Bars 137
Moist Brownies
Molasses Roll-Outs 138
"Monies" Sand Bakkels
Chewy Ginger Cookies
Snack Bars 139
Oatmeal Chocolate Chip
   Cookies
Oatmeal Macaroon Cookies
Peanut Butter Cups 140
Pumpkin Patch Cookies
Oatmeal Cookies
Peanut Butter Cookies................ 141
Pecan Bars
Pecan Pie Bars
Perfect Frosted Creams 142
Reese's Bars
Rice Krispie Balls
Rhubarb Cheesecake Bars 143
Rice Krispie Caramel Bars
Salted Nut Bars 144
Salted Nut Roll Bars
Snicker Bars
Sugar Cookie Bars 145
Triple Chocolate Brownie
   Cookies
Unbaked Shoestring Cookies
Whipped Cream Krumkake 146
Yum-Yum Brownies
Cooked Icing.............................. 147
Lemon Bars
Cake Mix Cookies
Peanut Butter Surprise 148
White Chip-Orange Dream
   Cookies................................. 149

Finish Line – Desserts

Speed Up Baking....................... 151
Apple Dumplings
Amazing Rhubarb Cobbler
American Berry No-Bake
   Cheesecake.......................... 152
Apple Crisp for One
Apple Dumpling Bake

Angel Food Dessert................... 153
Apple Upside-Down Cake
Black Russian Bundt Cake........ 154
Boston Cream Pie Loaf
Bread Pudding for Two 155
Broiler Cake
Brown Stone Front Cake
Brownie Cupcakes..................... 156
Brownie Trifle
Butterscotch Snack Cake
Caramel Dumplings................... 157
Caramel Ice Cream Sauce
Cherries and Cream Pie
Cherry-Pineapple Dessert 158
Chocolate Cake (2).................... 159
Chocolate Vinegar Cake
Cool and Creamy Coconut
   Cake 160
Chocolate Chip Cookie Mousse
Chocolate Pie 161
Cranberry Crisp
Creamy Lemon Pie
Daddy's Rice Pudding 162
Decadent Triple Layer Mud Pie
Daiquiri Dessert
Easy Dessert 163
Easy Lemon Dessert
Easy Rice Pudding 164
Fast Frostings
Fast Frosty Dessert Pie............. 165
Fluffy Frozen Peanut Butter Pie
Fresh Peach Pie
Frozen Berry Fluff...................... 166
Fruit Casserole
Hot Fudge Sauce (2) 167
Hurry-Up Luscious Angel Food
   Cake Topping
Ice Cream
Ice Cream Pie............................ 168
Irish Bread Pudding with
   Caramel Sauce
Good-To-Go Graham-Apple
   Stack-Ups 169
Grandma's Autumn Apple Cake
Granny's Peach Cobbler
Kids Quick Ice Cream................ 170
Lemon Bundt Cake

Lemon Cheesecake Dessert 171
Lemon Cream Dessert 172
Lemon Crumb Pie 173
Mama's Applesauce Cake
Mandarin Cake
Microwave Apple Crisp 174
Microwave Cherry Crisp
Mini Cheesecakes
Mini Upside-Down Pineapple
 Cakes 175
Missionary Cake
My Mom's Hot Fudge Sauce
No-Bake Lemon Cheesecake 176
Oatmeal Cake
Orange Cake 177
Orange Cake
Pineapple Dessert (2) 178
Pineapple Snow
Peppermint Ice Cream Cake 179
Pumpkin Pie Cake
Quick Cheesecake 180
Quick Fruit Pie
Rhubarb Cream Cake 181
Rhubarb Pie
Serving Pudding Cone
Kick-the-Can Ice Cream 182
Shaking Ice Cream 183

Sour Cream Cake with Sour
 Cream Filling
Smooth and Creamy Frosting 184
Speedy-Way Cranberry Pudding
7-Up Apple Dumplings 185
Strawberry Angel Delight 186
Strawberry Cheesecake Squares
 With Gingersnap Crust 187
Strawberry Frosting
Strawberry Pie 188
Strawberry Shortcut Cake
Swedish Apple Pie 189
Swedish Nut Cake
Triple Citrus Cheesecake 190
Yvette's Pumpkin Dessert 191

Tips & Tune-Ups

In The Kitchen 193-196
Around the House 196-199
Health 199
Outdoors 200
Potion for Deskunking the Dog
List of My Favorite
 Condiments 201
Something Special Added 202

NAME _____

ADDRESS _____

CITY & STATE _____ ZIP _____

How many?   Books available for order:

_____ North Dakota, Where Food is Love @ $15.00 (includes tax)
            P & H _____

_____ Season's Eatings from North Dakota @ $15.00 (includes tax)
            P & H _____

_____ Drive-By Cooking from North Dakota @ $15.00 (includes tax)
            P & H _____

Please make checks payable to: **Three Bears Honey Co.**

Send orders to: The Three Bears Honey Co.
                    908 63rd Ave. N.
                    Moorhead, MN 56560
                    218-236-5933

NAME _____

ADDRESS _____

CITY & STATE _____ ZIP _____

How many?   Books available for order:

_____ North Dakota, Where Food is Love @ $15.00 (includes tax)
            P & H _____

_____ Season's Eatings from North Dakota @ $15.00 (includes tax)
            P & H _____

_____ Drive-By Cooking from North Dakota @ $15.00 (includes tax)
            P & H _____

Please make checks payable to: **Three Bears Honey Co.**

Send orders to: The Three Bears Honey Co.
                    908 63rd Ave. N.
                    Moorhead, MN 56560
                    218-236-5933

NAME _____

ADDRESS _____

CITY & STATE _____ ZIP _____

How many?   Books available for order:

_____ North Dakota, Where Food is Love @ $15.00 (includes tax)
           P & H _____

_____ Season's Eatings from North Dakota @ $15.00 (includes tax)
           P & H _____

_____ Drive-By Cooking from North Dakota @ $15.00 (includes tax)
           P & H _____

Please make checks payable to: ***Three Bears Honey Co.***

Send orders to: The Three Bears Honey Co.
                    908 63rd Ave. N.
                    Moorhead, MN 56560
                    218-236-5933

— —

NAME _____

ADDRESS _____

CITY & STATE _____ ZIP _____

How many?   Books available for order:

_____ North Dakota, Where Food is Love @ $15.00 (includes tax)
           P & H _____

_____ Season's Eatings from North Dakota @ $15.00 (includes tax)
           P & H _____

_____ Drive-By Cooking from North Dakota @ $15.00 (includes tax)
           P & H _____

Please make checks payable to: ***Three Bears Honey Co.***

Send orders to: The Three Bears Honey Co.
                    908 63rd Ave. N.
                    Moorhead, MN 56560
                    218-236-5933